Capt. Raymond M
U.S. Navy (retired)

D0863251

PURPOSE!
The Forgotten Principle

with Foreword by
Vice Admiral Jim Stockdale
U.S. Navy (retired)

WITHDRAWN

DeWitt *Books*

Copyright 2000, by Raymond M. Wikstrom

**Publisher's Cataloging-in-Publication
(Provided by Quality Books, Inc.)**

Wikstrom, Raymond M
Purpose: the forgotten principle/Raymond M.
Wikstrom. -- 1st ed.
p. cm.
LCCN: 99-67998
ISBN: 0-9668231-2-5
1. United States--Moral conditions--20th
century. 2. Social values--United States.
3. Moral education--United States. I. Title

HD90.M6W55 2000   306'.0973
QB199-1738

Published by DeWitt Books
North Manchester, Indiana
http://www.dewittbooks.com

Printed in the United States of America by Eerdmans Printing

Cover design by TLC Graphics

ACKNOWLEDGMENTS

After 30 wonderful years in the United States Navy dedicating my career to the service of my country and 25 wonderful years devoting my love to my beautiful wife Gerry, who in turn raised our two extraordinary children while I was deployed, I have learned to appreciate that there is a purpose in life and that God is at the center of it. If you surround God with your family, friends, neighbors, and workmates, value their worth and support your community and your country as a patriot, you will surely have lived a purposeful life. If you truly want to feel good about yourself, just pour an elixir of morality, patriotism and love into a beaker and mix thoroughly, and I guarantee you will enjoy this recipe of life.

I must acknowledge the inspirational courage of a true American hero in Vice Admiral James Stockdale, a naval aviator, a prisoner-of-war, and a nationally recognized leader who was very kind indeed to write the foreword to my book.

In addition, I must also acknowledge Worth Weller for his support in giving me the opportunity to publish this book by DeWitt Books of Indiana. His superb editing and tremendous insight as a journalist and author, enabled me to successfully complete a book of values that I believe have been missing over the past few decades.

And finally, to my father, Floyd Wikstrom, who along with my mother Cecelia, raised two sons with the proper amount of love and discipline which enabled us to possess the right values and the courage of our convictions to become whatever we wanted to become. I will always cherish their wisdom and love.

PURPOSE:
THE FORGOTTEN PRINCIPLE

TABLE OF CONTENTS

*"We were not here to
cope, or languish, or sit out the
war, or 'be reasonable.' And
we pledged to 'stick it in their
ear,' to keep it up, no matter
how long we stayed."*
**James Stockdale
from the Medal of
Honor Winner's bestselling
book, *In Love and War,*
about his years as a POW
in Hanoi.**

Foreword

Ray Wikstrom is a very honest, forthright, and purposeful man. He is the husband of a loving and loyal wife, father of their 21-year-old son and a younger daughter preparing to enter college—a family much like mine, brought up with Dad often at sea, a career U.S. Naval Officer. Recently retired from the Navy, Ray has poured his mind, heart and soul into this very thorough and readable discourse about our national purposes, both moral and political.

Ray writes from personal conviction; and what he writes in this book of values has everything to do with what he hopes will be his readers' soul-searching thought as we approach this first national election of the 21st century. He thinks there is a lot of work to be done to get the country back on a sane track, and I agree with him.

I first met Ray in the fall of 1989 when in the office of the head of the United States Navy, in Washington, D.C.

He and his family were there to celebrate his being awarded the James Bond Stockdale Inspirational Leadership Award.

There are two winners of this award every year, each in the rank of commander, one from the Pacific and one from the Atlantic Fleet. Each must be serving at the time as a commanding officer of a destroyer, an aviation squadron, or a submarine. Ray was then commander of an Atlantic Fleet aviation squadron, and his counterpart, Commander T. B. Fargo, was commanding officer of a Pacific Fleet submarine. The award itself is an elaborate bronze casting. Each winner receives one.

That year of 1989 was the ninth time the award was presented. The next presentation, in the fall of 2000, will be the 20th.

This award was established by the Secretary of the Navy when physical disability from combat wounds in Vietnam brought about my retirement from active duty in 1979. I was given carte blanche authority to set forth its zone of eligibility and requirements for receiving it. I wanted its recipients to be right at the "jumping off point" for distinguished careers, and from experience I knew that the Commanders of seagoing commands were the perfect pool for aspiring senior leaders.

I had a burning concern about this award, which I had limited to just two selectees a year, as the award steadily gained prestige from the time it was announced, thinking it could nicely use a "grass roots" readout to deflect the selection of "front office aides" to the detriment of salt water sailors. I requested of the Secretary of the Navy that he approve my idea of having the requirement of "peer nomination" be mandatory for all finalists prior to their names getting into the hat before the official "selection board" in Washington for the Stockdale award. He ordered it so, and it has been a very successful hedge against what I feared. The crowbar for getting one's name into the hat before the selection board is not the application, but the spontaneous letter of recommendation from a fellow commanding officer eligible, but not competing to receive the same award.

The Stockdale award is the only Navy award dependent on peer nomination.

I pressed for this remembering how when as an aircraft squadron commander I and many of my peers shook our heads when we saw top level jobs going to the wrong people. It always makes me feel safer when the Stockdale Award contenders list comes out each spring, knowing that each nominee had a friend who laid his reputation on the line in recommending in so many words, "He is at least as good and maybe a better man than I." This also pumps a shot of altruism into a boiling pot of competition—something the Navy can use.

That Ray Wikstrom shows all the characteristics of a natural, courageous and talented leader goes without saying. He flew 666 combat missions in Vietnam between October 1969 and October 1970. He flew four types of helicopters (H-1 Huey Gunships in Vietnam; H-2 Sea Sprites from the decks of fast frigates and cruisers; H-3's from carrier decks; and H-60 Seahawks in a training environment). After receiving the Stockdale Award, Ray Wikstrom went on to be assigned to four more commands at sea: another aviation squadron; a Helicopter Wing consisting of five squadrons; and two deep draft ship commands, the USS Okinawa and the USS Tarawa. He fought in combat in two wars, Vietnam and Desert Storm.

I quote from his writings, as a measure of the man and Naval Officer that he is: "Leading 1,600 Sailors and Marines aboard the USS Okinawa (LPH-3) during combat operations in the Persian Gulf War was an experience that few will ever encounter and that I will never forget. The responsibility for the lives of these men and the trust the Navy placed in my leadership to guide them was truly an honor that I humbly will cherish throughout my life."

And that he is a serious, thoughtful thinker, writing with the best interests of his beloved country at heart, is amply illustrated by his first book, *Purpose: The Forgotten Principle.*

Read Ray Wikstrom's book and learn what you can do to make your family stronger, your life more meaningful, and your country a better democracy.

Vice Admiral Jim Stockdale, U.S. Navy (retired)
February, 2000
Coronado, California

"Hold faithfulness and sincerity
as first principles. "
Confucius, 551 - 479 B.C.

Introduction

I am an ordinary citizen of the United States of America. Or at least I believe I am.

Now in my early fifties, I recently retired from the military in time to pursue a second career that doesn't take me away from my family. My wife and I have two children, a son in college and a daughter in high school. We have been happily married for more than 25 years. We feel good about that.

Early in life I learned from my parents about right and wrong, truth and falsehood, kindness and cruelty. I go to church regularly, but don't consider myself a member of the religious right. I abide by the law whether I agree with it or not, with the exception of occasionally speeding (yes, I am a little impatient at times).

I do understand other points of view, but I don't feel compelled to always agree. And I speak out loudly against ideas and behaviors I tolerate but do not condone, especially if they are immoral, illegal, lack a common sense of decency or don't conform to established community standards.

After listening to both sides of the debate, I have chosen to be a conservative on most issues. I am also a disciplinarian (just ask my children). I taught them right from wrong. I taught them about morals and ethics and principles and values. I ensured that they understood these beliefs to be the bedrock foundation for their personal views on life, liberty and the pursuit of happiness. In short, I showed them the *purpose* of life.

This is the basis from which I now write.

After having raised two children in this way and commanded thousands of sailors in this fashion, I find it troubling that many American citizens fail to understand this basic notion of purpose in their daily lives. Many, it seems, have trouble detecting right from wrong, truth from lie, and kindness from cruelty. Apparently these words no longer have a commonly understood meaning. Their meaning, for some at least, seems to be only that which is personally expedient at the moment.

A good portion of the citizenry today no longer effectively uses the English language, due to a lack of sufficient higher-level vocabulary skills. It is these skills, coupled with a basic notion of good and evil, that allow you to become a critical thinker, helping you successfully analyze the purpose of events occurring around you.

I wonder just how many Americans can actually define morals and ethics, principles and values? These words are important for they are not just words, they are a guiding philosophy—a set of values, ideas and opinions which reflect a way of life that many Americans cherish. Therefore, I believe that if you cannot define these words, if you do not understand what they mean or how they reflect upon the notion of right and wrong, you in fact do not understand the purpose for them in society.

This much is clear: everything we do or say, or hear or see in our daily life, is done or said or heard or seen with a specific intent and purpose behind it. But do we really understand those intents and purposes, or are we simply slaves to the views of professional spin-doctors? Are we merely parroting their comments and imitating their actions? Haven't we failed to thoroughly analyze the real purpose behind their pithy utterances?

I believe that many Americans in the United States today are not well enough educated to determine the true intent or purpose behind the things that are said and done in society. They are simply motivated by what they are told through spin, advertising and simplistic--even duplicitous--rhetoric.

Many lack the critical thinking skills necessary to determine the difference between truth and spin. Or--an even worse case scenario--many are simply too lazy and don't care. They miss the real meaning of events because they fail to thoroughly analyze the situation. They rely on others to do the analysis for them. They refuse to do the research. They blindly accept as gospel what they hear and see on radio and television or what they read in newspapers and magazines.

Admittedly, there are opposing and conflicting views on just about every topic today. For example, just when you have finally weaned yourself from fried eggs for breakfast you learn that eggs are actually good for you!

These constant contradictions should make it even more important that we search out the truth and conduct a little critical thinking for ourselves. There is no other way to dispel the confusion.

I am, to say the least, disturbed with the failure of fortitude displayed by many Americans in resolving our ethical and civil disputes. It is as if we as a nation have given up our principles because holding true appears to be a losing battle. We would rather look the other way than go to the effort to take a stand that we know is right but which might upset the apple cart. On the flip side of that sad old song, it appears that for many, blind loyalty to a cause, no matter the apparent contradiction, is more important for advancing the agenda than acting on principle to defend the notion of right and wrong.

Our media tend to focus on the absurd, the tragedies and the ugliness in society rather than the norm, the celebrations and the good. I would much rather read about the dedicated, local heroes who organize the neighborhood to find a lost child than to read about the crazed motivations of the kidnapper after the mutilated body of the child is found. I would much rather read about the celebrations of marriage, birth, graduation or achievement than the tragedy caused by two demented youths in Columbine High School in Littleton, Colorado. I would much rather watch a wholesome television show encompassing morality, love and respect for one another than watch the kinky, absurd and distorted demonstrations on the Jerry Springer Show. I doubt that I am alone in these preferences.

Unfortunately we have accepted as the norm these gory details of life rather than understanding that although these are indeed life's tragedies, there are also 270 million other American stories to be told that don't reflect this kind of sensationalism. The media have nationalized local issues to the point of actually intruding on the personal lives of the victims of these horrendous crimes against humanity, apparently for the sole purpose of exciting our emotions. The constant replay of these horrific and emotional scenes has convinced the populace that these are widespread occurrences throughout the land, when in fact they are not. Why else--other than by a crude effort to attract more advertising--would the network and cable television stations nationalize the funerals of all the victims of the Columbine High School massacre? At every tragedy, TV monitors capture these raw emotions. No wonder we all feel helpless.

This kind of sensationalism needs to stop. We are allowing our emotions to take over our senses. One could believe — and some do — that these school shootings indicate America is doomed. Yet how many other schools in our nation or even our own cities have not had any school shootings to report?

We need to get a grip on our perspective and use our critical thinking skills, rather than our emotions, to solve problems. We need to be more involved in local issues rather than get incensed over broader issues we can do nothing about.

We need to lift ourselves out of the gutter.

I suggest there is another way to approach the cultural war in our society, and that is to examine the intent and purpose behind the numerous influences affecting our daily lives. We need to understand and continually reevaluate the messages with which our culture bombards us every day, seeking out their true purpose.

I believe we as a nation are at a crossroads. The majority of average Americans expect their peers and their leaders to display a true spirit of morality, family values and common, decent standards. They are tired of being ignored, spurned and ridiculed by those in our society who prefer to disregard the rule of law or any connection to moral or ethical behavior.

I believe we need to reexamine our souls in this regard. It is time to take a fresh approach to evaluating the intents and purposes of the rules and regulations of government and society that structure our daily living and determine how we interact with one another.

The task is not that hard. Have you ever heard of the old lawyerly phrase "for all intents and purposes," or the sibling response, "Mom, Mikey did it on purpose"? That's what I'm talking about, the intent and purpose behind the things we see, say and do.

In the following pages I will attempt to examine how losing sight of purposes has caused our society to become out of control. Without purpose we lack self-discipline, resulting in our becoming uncivil and uncaring toward one another.

The outstanding economy has been both a boon and a bane to our well-being. The fervent pursuit of wealth in the late '80s and throughout the '90s has distracted us. These relatively easy times have allowed us to regard money and good times as more important than purpose of belief.

I contend, as I will illustrate in the following chapters, that our societal drifting can be attributed to a failure to understand the intentions, good or bad, of our fellow man. To me it is all based upon...*PURPOSE: The Forgotten Principle!*.

"He was wont to speak plain and to the purpose."
Shakespeare:
Much Ado About Nothing

Chapter 1: The Purpose of Purpose

Definition of Purpose: An intended or desired result, goal or aim; resolve.

I have been convinced for some time now that America has lost its way. We have neglected those very morals and ethics and principles and values I had assumed were the most precious gift I could pass on to my children.

We no longer regard a lack of morals as a family shame or even a community tragedy. It just doesn't matter to some.

Equally as disturbing, we no longer value the rights of the family or those of larger groups. Rather, the rights of the individual are paramount to collective rights, no matter the standard established by the group or society. Our philosophy of ethics now depends upon one's personal

point of view. It is often not grounded in honorable
principles or purposes. Reasonable people may reasonably
disagree on the value of certain ideas, but one thing we
must all agree on is the notion of right and wrong. To
have a society that continues as a viable culture, we must
adhere to common standards of decency and behavior.
We must possess the integrity to do what is right and not
just what is expedient or what feels good.

We must reevaluate the intent and purpose as to why
we do things, recognizing that without standards we cannot
properly make value judgments.

Many people in America today refuse to get involved.
They prefer not to be judgmental of someone's behavior or
words. They would rather look the other way than tell
their best friends that their behavior is outlandish, reckless
or immoral. In other words, why risk the loss of a friend
over something as silly as imprudent behavior. "Everybody
does it." Right?

Wrong. Not everybody does it, nor does everyone
condone it.

It is amazing to me that the liberal left refuses to
acknowledge that it is judgmental of word or deed, when
in fact we are clearly a nation that is judgmental. Almost
everything we do requires us to form an opinion, make a
decision, or estimate a value. When we form an opinion,
or make a decision, or estimate a value, what we are really
doing is making a judgment based upon a set of standards
we think should be used for comparison. Of course these
standards may vary, as may the value we place upon them,
but you cannot deny the fact that a judgment is required
no matter the standard. Therefore, to say we cannot make
a judgment of someone's behavior or character is to deny
the truth that we all do make judgments every day.

For better or for worse, we are judgmental!

For example, when you decide to let your son drive his buddies to a high school football game, you consider many things in your decision to allow him the use of the family car. What is the distance he will drive? What time is the game? Who are his friends? When do they plan on coming home? Is there a party after the game? And if so, where is it? Could alcohol be involved? These judgmental decisions are important if you care about the welfare of your son.

When you make a business decision, you often decide whether or not to trust the person you are dealing with. Do I require a down payment just in case? Will a handshake suffice versus a written contract? Should I get the advice of a lawyer?

Every decision we make requires a judgment to be made. Every opinion we form requires that we judge the situation based upon a set of standards we personally possess.

The same is true of behavior. There are many people who are simply unwilling to publicly make a judgment of somebody's behavior because they have bought into the so often quoted phrase, "Who are you to play God? Who are you to judge what is right or wrong about my behavior?"

Interesting comments considering many refuse to invoke God unless it serves their particular purpose. In fact, they simply do not want to admit the truth about their behavior, even if it falls below a certain standard for which they are unwilling to accept from their own families.

Why then do many people not commit themselves to be judgmental about public figures, but are quite willing to do so with their family? As I have previously mentioned, they refuse to get involved because they do not understand the intent and purpose of standards for a civil society and why we should enforce them.

Without such standards, discipline breaks down, trust

disintegrates, tempers flare and civility is lost. Without a common standard for comparison, anything goes. Therefore, it is necessary to develop trust to restore civility, which will only be restored when we are sincere in our efforts to be completely honest in our actions and our words. We must understand the purpose and value of a standard. That is, we need to recognize the intended result of a worthwhile and accepted principle of comparison.

As the nation enters the third millennium since the birth of Christ, we Americans, of all colors and ethnicity, need to understand what was behind the Founding Father's belief that America should be a society consisting of citizens with certain principles and inalienable rights. I firmly believe that the Founding Fathers viewed these rights as collective rights. They are not simply the rights of lonely individuals, but rather are shared rights—almost obligations to each other.

Although there have been many turbulent times throughout our 224 years as a nation, we have persevered as a free people, because we have long believed that our rights as citizens outweigh both those of the state and those as solitary individuals. Hence, we have voluntarily, for the most part, subjected ourselves to a military draft, taxation and a host of other measures that to some degree restrict our freedom but which in the long run keep us free as a nation.

However, it's no secret that all is not well.

As industry and technology developed over the past two centuries, our nation prospered. With new prosperity came many new challenges as people developed new ideas, started new businesses and entered into new technology-driven enterprises. But as the nation grew in size and the number of Americans multiplied, it became much more difficult for the government to interact with the daily lives of ordinary citizens. Representative democracy became less representational.

Today, our government—now really comprised of a diverse array of special interest groups—has gone far beyond the purpose our Founding Fathers intended. Lobbyists and a veritable army of bureaucratic staffers have become surrogate representatives. They—not we—drive the agenda. Power, not principle, drives the government. Our representatives have too often assaulted the purpose of principles for which America was founded, doing instead the bidding of the activists, lobbyists and self-serving staffers to retain their power.

We have gotten too big. We have lost our way.

We need to read or reread the Constitution of the United States, the *Federalists' Papers* and the *Declaration of Independence* to understand what we are all about as a nation. We need to understand the concept of intent and purpose.

Far too often we fail to question the real reason we do things. We either take our actions for granted, or we assume they are done for the right reasons. Sometimes our excuse is simply that we've always done it that way in the past. Often we are just too lazy to invest the time and energy in trying to determine if this is the best we can do.

In short, we never challenge the notion of purpose.

Think about it.

Why did we establish a federal government for our nation two centuries ago with an Executive, Legislative and Judicial branch as coequal partners in governing? Why did we also establish additional layers of state, county and city governments?

Why did we establish a mandatory public school system? Why do we establish private organizations and associations which only cater to like-minded people? Why, for that matter, do we establish any organization or activity in our society?

The answers to these questions will invariably differ. We all have our own opinions, some based in fact and others based in assumption. However, the challenge for us ought to be to at least question the intent and purpose behind the reason for establishing governments, school systems and private organizations. Do they still function as we desire them to function? Are all their associated rules, regulations and mandates still appropriate? Are their charters still relevant? Should their bylaws be amended?

In other words, what is the intent and purpose for their existence?

We are regularly presented with an overwhelming number of issues that require a concentrated, intelligent response. Whether the issues are posed as a question or presented as a fact, our first thought ought to be to determine the purpose behind them. If you can understand their purpose—why they were said or done—then you can be reasonably assured that your responses to them will be with some purpose of thought.

That doesn't mean it is the only response, nor necessarily the right response. But it will be an appropriate response if it is backed by the principles of right or wrong, based on morality, ethics and legal standing. Without these bedrock principles of right and wrong, we cannot understand the purpose for which the question, or issue was presented.

Take for example, the death penalty. This obviously is a highly polarized subject—one so polarized that many on the same side of other volatile issues disagree on this one. Even the religious right can't agree on the purpose of the death penalty.

My own view is pretty straightforward. The death penalty was enacted by state legislatures for the very purpose of ridding the populace of the most dangerous people in our society—people who have perpetrated the most horrendous of crimes against humanity. These are people who lack, for what ever reason, the basic ethics required to live in a civilized society. Because it is extremely difficult to inculcate morality on a mind that lacks a fundamental sense of right and wrong, the death penalty may be the only appropriate remedy.

Of course, not everyone would agree with my view. There are many who think rehabilitation does work, or that a life sentence is better than the death penalty anytime. For after all, who are we to be judgmental? Why should we play God?

I have no argument with these people.

On the other hand, there are some who believe that the death penalty is a deterrent to other like-minded people intent on murder. But I believe the death penalty, if carried out swiftly without numerous delays and appeals, is appropriate for certain crimes because it is intended to rid the populace of the person who has committed a heinous crime for which he alone is accountable.

Although many claim the death sentence serves to deter future felons from committing murder, I don't believe this was the purpose for which it was enacted in the first place.

To me, it is all about accountability. The murderer should be held accountable for his actions to society, just as he is held accountable to God for his repentance and salvation.

Therefore, regardless of whether you accept my view of the purpose of the death penalty, the challenges for you are to examine its purpose and determine whether it is relevant in today's society.

I happen to think it is.

But the point to be made is that regardless of ideology, we need to examine the *purpose* behind our words, actions and views.

*"Standards are always out
of date. That is what makes
them standards."*
**Alan Bennett, 1934-
(English actor and dramatist)**

Chapter 2: The
Purpose of Standards

*The purpose of standards is to provide an
acceptable basis for comparison.*

For better or for worse, standards are a standard
part of our existence.

We have standards for graduation from high school,
standards for ethical behavior in government, standards
for participation in sports, standards of conduct in the
workplace, standards for dress, standards for conducting
meetings, standards for entering military service, just to
name a few. We live our daily routines by following
standards of behavior.

But many standards do not remain standard for long.
We change standards all the time, sometimes in response
to changes in our society and other times for more arbitrary

reasons. Sometimes we raise the bar. Sometimes we lower the bar. Sometimes the bar remains in place while we introduce subtle adjustments that in effect change the basis for comparison.

Let me provide you with some examples.

The state of Virginia recently introduced new Standards of Learning examinations given to public school students. The initial results of these statewide tests indicated a dramatic decline in the number of students who passed, compared to previous statewide testing. In fact, many principals and teachers were disturbed by these new results. Did they mean the tests were too hard? Should the state reevaluate the newly formed standards? Or should they continue with the effort to improve public education?

As you might imagine, there were many viewpoints on this subject. Not all were happy. The standards changed: the bar in this case was raised, thus lowering the scores.

Raising educational standards is a good thing in my opinion, if we want to fix the poor showing of American education throughout the world. Other states should do the same. After all, what is the purpose of education? Isn't it to improve students' knowledge so that they can compete in the marketplace, make a decent living and become productive citizens? Isn't it the only guarantee that our citizens of tomorrow will be able to live enriched, full lives?

If we agree that the purpose of education is highly valued, then why do we continue to accept the current dismal graduation rates?

American public education has one of the worst records among the industrialized nations in the world. High school students around the nation have been allowed to graduate without the requisite knowledge to perform well in today's workplace. Many require remedial courses prior to entering college.

How sad is that?

What this suggests to me is that we have not met the purpose of education as a whole in our society. We have abrogated our responsibility to many of the children of this nation.

I'm not pointing my finger, because there is plenty of blame to go around. Ill-prepared students and teachers, the failure by school administrators to enforce strict standards , soft curriculum, apathetic parents—these are all fundamental ingredients of this awful tasting stew.

The point should be to find a solution. Is it more money? More discipline? Longer hours? Smaller classrooms? Tougher standards? Changes in the curriculum? Back to basics? All of the above?

This long overdue debate needs serious consideration. We need to finally put the children first in the debate and discount the desires of the teachers' unions and other organizations and political opportunists that are endorsing their own particular agendas at the expense of the kids.

The purpose of mandatory public school education is to ensure a safe environment in which all students learn the basics to compete in life after high school. If that requires enforcing discipline, ensuring minimum standards to graduate, or not allowing students to participate in extracurricular activities or sports unless those minimum standards are met, then so be it.

We often hear from students or their parents, that there is too much homework assigned, which interferes with after-school jobs or extracurricular activities.

Well, so what? What activities are we talking about? Have they joined too many clubs? Do they need the job to make ends meet, or are they simply earning money to buy name brand clothes? Parents need to determine what is more important to the well being of our children after they graduate from high school. We need to understand the purpose and benefit of each extracurricular activity or job, and then make an informed decision on whether the benefits outweigh those of our children's mandatory education. We cannot let them join every club and play sports and then claim that they don't have time for their homework.

We need to stop the coaches who seek "soft" courses for their students, to ensure they remain academically eligible to participate in sports. Principals who feel the graduation rates for the student body as a whole (to make the school look better) are more important than the individual grade point average of each student need to be removed.

We ought to insist on certain minimum standards and stick to them. If we do that, and remain consistent, then coaches and teachers and students will understand the rules and will be forced to comply.

If the parents, teachers and coaches aren't concerned with standards, then why do we expect the students to care? Adults need to take charge and enforce the standards. After all, the purpose of education does not require that all students play sports or join every club imaginable.

Why do we continue to coddle every parental, student or coach's desire for his own personal preferences, rather than insisting upon minimum school standards for graduation to the next level? Is the authorities' allegiance in this regard in the best interest of their students? Or are the school administrators, principals, teachers and coaches simply trying to get through the day as easily as possible? Is their goal graduation for each student regardless of his or her knowledge level, or is their job to teach students the basics so they can meet the minimum standards of graduation?

Private and parochial schools on average have far superior graduation rates, and the number of college-bound graduates are noteworthy compared to public schools. I am definitely not suggesting that all of us send our children to private or parochial schools. I am suggesting, however, that these schools must be doing something right.

What is the difference in the purpose of education between private and public schools? There shouldn't be any difference in their purpose. Both should be providing safe learning environments to help students master the basic educational standards so that they can successfully support themselves after graduation and lead enriched lives. Yes, some private schools have additional purposes: to teach morality, military training, discipline and the like. But you cannot deny that they are fulfilling their charters. If they didn't, they would go out of business.

Another example where we have lowered the bar (but raised the scores) is in the adjusted scores for the Scholastic Aptitude Tests given to college-bound students. Several years ago, the raw scores were increased, apparently to compensate for what some claimed were racial biases in the testing. I have found that hard to fathom. In any case, raising the SAT raw scores only made the students (and schools) feel better about their accomplishments. It had little to do with improving education. Just because you raise the scores does not a smarter student make!

So what have we accomplished?

Prestigious schools still require students to compete for scholarships and entrance to their various programs. Artificially raising the SAT scores gives false hope to those graduating high school students who now think that they can compete with others in their class for prestigious programs. So, what was the *purpose* in adjusting the SAT scores for college-bound students? Your guess is as good as mine.

I am not arguing against raising or lowering standards. (As I previously mentioned, we continuously change standards.) Rather, I am trying to defend the idea that we ought to challenge the purpose for changing the standard.

Even worse than raising or lowering the bar is to subtly change the basis of comparison. This essentially changes the dynamic in measuring the standard.

Many people are never aware that this takes place.

For example, affirmative action in college and university enrollment has not changed the level of the bar. It has simply made quotas available for certain selected groups of individuals based upon skin color or other characteristics that do not necessarily reflect merit. The public myth—fading fast—is that students selected on the basis of quotas have actually competed and won on merit. This we know is a fraud! What has actually happened is that the standards have been lowered to let certain selected groups of individuals who do not meet the standards every other individual must meet, enroll in prestigious schools.

You might ask why this is wrong. It is wrong because it causes some students who have met the standards legitimately to be denied the (competitive) right to attend school because a different—and lower—standard was applied for some and not for others.

There are many people who suggest that standards need to be flexible. I agree, and often they are. The obvious problem with flexible standards, however, is that the bar moves up or down depending upon who is doing the hiring or placing or selecting. In other words, it depends upon someone's judgment.

There it is again, that dreaded word: *judgment*. Sometimes a selection is made based upon the whole person—leadership traits, working experience, character or extracurricular activities—and not necessarily only upon high school or college level grade point averages or class ranking. And that's the way it ought to be.

I did not mention physical characteristics as a standard because I believe that it should not matter what pigment your skin is or what your gender is. I should hire you or admit you based upon established minimum acceptable standards AND what you can bring to the organization based upon the whole person concept. But, we must have some minimum acceptable standard, or otherwise the hiring, firing, placing and selecting would be solely based upon arbitrary judgment. This would be disastrous, because merit would lose out to the good 'ole boy network more often than not.

The idea of establishing standards is not new. They have been around a long, long time. We recognize we need standards to ensure that desired, predictable results are obtained.

Many standards are set in the form of regulations and laws. Some are more palatable than others.

For example, we insist upon stricter standards with a greater degree of enforcement when it affects our public safety. Whether we're talking about random inspection of meat and other food processing activities, limits on passenger aircraft and engine operating times as well as aircrew flying hours, or physical endurance and strength standards required of soldiers, police officers and fire fighters, the public demands their safety first.

It appears we take seriously the government's intervention into regulating our lives when it comes to our medical and physical well-being. We are ready to sue if we get ill over tainted meat, or get injured in an aircraft mishap, or claim the police didn't respond soon enough to protect us from crime.

But what about other regulations imposed upon us by the government, such as traffic safety standards, or boating safety standards, or—heaven forbid—gun control standards? We don't necessarily like the government to intervene in these areas because we consider vehicles, boats and guns our personal property. Therefore, we might feel, they should not be regulated.

We are not entirely happy when the government sets these kinds of standards for us.

Nevertheless, we don't complain very loudly about registering our private boats and cars; yet we find particularly offensive any suggestion to register our private firearms because many conservatives claim the Constitution guarantees us the right to bear arms. Any attempt at regulation, even for the safety of the general public, results in a charge that we are tampering with private property and denigrating our constitutional rights.

At this point, however, I say, *WAIT A SECOND!*

Those who claim it's none of the government's business when it comes to regulating personal property, such as registering handguns, or insisting on mandatory use of seatbelt and child restraint devices in our own vehicles, or requiring we comply with established boating rules and regulations in our own boats, just don't understand that private ownership is not the issue. The issue is *public safety.*

Why then do we make a distinction between public and private concerns when our safety is at stake?

I believe it is because we detest regulations that infringe upon our personal freedom. Many citizens would rather accept the risk of injury or death than have their private life regulated.

That notion, I believe, is misplaced when it infringes upon the safety of the general population. I don't think we are as concerned about personal freedom as much as we are concerned about our private lives being inconvenienced.

However, we no longer live in a society that is private. We cannot go anywhere today without crossing from our private boundaries into the public domain. We cannot use highways and boat ramps and airports without crossing into the public arena. We cannot go shopping, eat at restaurants or go to the movies without mixing our personal or private outings with the general public. We are no longer an unregulated frontier nation.

Therefore, I do not understand the logic that says we can register our cars, and we can register our boats, but we cannot register our guns because they are personal property. I'm not suggesting we do away with private gun ownership, neither am I suggesting that we do away with private automobiles or boats. But I am a firm believer that one of the highest priorities of government is to protect its citizens. Therefore, I believe that regulation of firearms falls into this category and is a valid concern for government intervention.

The point to remember is that the purpose of these regulations is to protect the public, *not* to restrict personal freedom. Critics of course will say that it should be their right to own a gun without restriction and to ride in their own automobile without a seatbelt. But personally, I have no problem being inconvenienced by registering a gun, or wearing a seatbelt that statistics have proven saves lives.

The government attempts to regulate safety in most cases to ensure certain standards are met, such as vehicle emission standards or properly working headlights and brakes, or for certifying professional and recreational licenses in order to protect the public's interest. So again, why the distinction between the regulated demands for public safety standards, yet a "hands off" approach to other safety concerns when it affects private property?

An argument may be made that we have too much

regulation, and therefore, too much licensing and registration. That's an issue we need to discuss with our city, state and federal representatives. We need to review the breadth and scope and purpose of these regulations to determine if they are still viable.

But how do we manage public resources such as hunting preserves, fishing holes, local beaches and other public property without standards and regulations? It is a necessary burden for the good of society. Without standardization and regulation, our natural resources would soon be depleted.

For example, we often complain here in Florida that on the one hand the public beaches are too crowded and unsafe to support four wheel drive vehicles and the public simultaneously, so we demand intervention to ease the crowding. But then on the other hand we don't understand why we've banned four wheel drive vehicles on the same beach for safety reasons when it interferes with our personal freedom to do our thing.

The difference of course, is that driving your private four-wheel drive vehicle on a crowded public beach is not a *property* issue, it is a *safety* issue.

Similarly, avid motorcyclists also claim they should have the right to decide whether to wear a helmet while riding on the streets and highways. Again, is this a personal property issue or a safety issue on a public thoroughfare? Should we require motorcyclists to carry the necessary insurance to pay their hospital bills should they have a mishap? If not and they carry no insurance, then is it the taxpayer's responsibility to foot their hospital bills?

I think not.

But back to my previous point about understanding the purpose of standards and regulations.

Although I am a conservative, it is difficult for me to

follow the logic proposed by the National Rifle Association and others against registering of handguns and requiring gun safety locks. To me this is a safety issue pure and simple. It does not infringe upon the right of citizens to bear arms.

The right to bear arms was enacted before America had a standing army, when militias were necessary for common defense against enemies. That was their purpose.

Today I think it is an emotional smokescreen by many conservatives to use the threat that gun control for safety reasons somehow undermines our constitutional rights. Some liberals use a similar smokescreen to insist that the Constitution requires the separation of church and state and therefore no mention of God is permitted in a public forum.

Both are an inaccurate—maybe even dishonest— interpretation of the Constitution. If you have absolutely nothing to hide and are a law-abiding citizen, if you are secure in your faith and aren't trying to push yours on anyone else, then where is the threat to your freedom?

Gun manufacturers ought to fully embrace safety measures because just as the tobacco companies have been blamed for not protecting smokers, they too may lose the fight over recent lawsuits for their perceived lack of protecting victims of gun violence.

But don't misunderstand me, I don't believe for one minute that the tobacco companies or the gun manufacturers are guilty of any crimes. It is the consumers and users who are responsible for their own actions. But big cities with their hosts of greedy lawyers are out for big bucks.

We need to keep in mind the purpose of gun control. It is not, as some maintain, a vast conspiracy to infringe upon the right to own guns. It's a safety issue for the general public.

The dividing line between private and public is not as

sharp as it once was. We can no longer survive in our private worlds without entering the public domain. Once we enter the public domain, we should expect to be asked to adhere to standards for the common good, particularly when the public perceives that safety is the issue.

Consequently, I have trouble with people who demand they be allowed to carry guns across private boundaries to public highways and byways, and then expect not to be regulated by standards that are set for the good of the public.

The argument that felons and others intent on criminal behavior don't worry about regulations is another smokescreen. We license automobiles, yet they still get stolen, misused and cause deaths. Should we stop licensing drivers and cars because not everybody complies?

No, the reason we have laws in the first place is to provide standards that are set for the common good.

Again, I'm not suggesting that guns be banned, nor am I advocating for laws against carrying a concealed weapon. Rather, I am suggesting that for the good of society in general, we should set standards for private property in the public domain if their purpose affects safety issues. The *purpose* of these standards would be to ensure the public's safety, *not* to restrict the public's freedom.

*"We make out of the
quarrel with others, rhetoric,
but of the quarrel with ourselves, poetry."*
W. B. Yeats

Chapter 3: The Purpose of Rhetoric

***The purpose of rhetoric is to effectively use
language to persuade others to your point of view.***

All of us, every day, use our language skills to
converse with friends, neighbors, business partners and
customers. We try to be persuasive. We want our point of
view heard and accepted.

If we are not persuasive, we lose the debate.

Sometimes we lose the debate because we have not
mastered the use of language (poor schooling perhaps).
Sometimes we lose the debate because the other point of
view is far more compelling (they have the facts on their
side). And sometimes we lose the debate because the other
side has used rhetoric that is dishonest—rhetoric that is
not meant to inform but which has as its only *purpose* the
goal of winning at any cost.

Being persuasive requires that we know what we are talking about and can convey our idea in an intelligent manner. Persuasion should—but doesn't always—entail that we be honest in our evaluation of the facts at our disposal.

We all know that there are many people who are not fully honest in their dealings with one another. These people prefer to manipulate language to their benefit, and often they win the debate in this manner.

Please don't misunderstand me. I'm not suggesting that we should not use language vigorously, even aggressively at times. Rather, I am urging that our rhetoric be honest, at all times.

Dishonest rhetoric goes to the heart of integrity. I believe this is why we have forgotten how to be civil with one another regarding our use of the English language: we fail to speak with integrity

Americans, according to the polls, are fed up with politicians, lawyers, and others who use outrageous and dishonest language in an attempt to fraudulently promote their point of view. We have not forgotten that words have consequences when spoken or written, yet sometimes we seem surprised when these consequences are incivility at best and violence at worst.

For example, during the impeachment and trial of President Bill Clinton in the House and the Senate, many of us observed on television some of the most ridiculous rhetoric imaginable. It was bombastic (pompous), it was dishonest (parsing of words), and it was clearly uncivil (rude). Instead of focusing on the purpose of the hearing, many of these intelligent politicians attacked each other's motives, the Independent Counsel, the Chairman, the counselors on either side, or the process itself. Anything to avoid addressing the issue at hand.

We may not like the fact that the President of the

United States was undergoing an impeachment hearing and trial, but we should understand its *purpose*. The purpose of these events was to adhere to a law passed by Congress in the wake of Watergate some 25 years ago.

The Independent Counsel statute required that the Justice Department look into allegations of wrongful abuse by the President. Attorney General Janet Reno requested that a three-judge federal panel in Washington, D.C. appoint an independent counsel to look into these matters. Judge Starr was appointed as the Independent Counsel, and after winning several motions from the Supreme Court and other federal district judges, he put forth his findings to the Judiciary Committee of the House of Representatives. The full House voted out two articles of impeachment and forwarded them to the Senate for trial. The Senate, in nearly an even split of votes on both articles, found the President not guilty. The impeachment articles failed to garner the two-thirds (67) vote required for conviction and removal, according to the constitutional process.

Pretty straightforward in retrospect.

But the story, as played out on television, was considerably more convoluted than that. Hard to ignore was the bombastic, dishonest rhetoric obviously designed to persuade the members of Congress to vote one way or the other.

Much of the disgusting rhetoric displayed during the House Judiciary Committee hearings had nothing to do with the facts of the case.

Congresswoman Maxine Waters, for example, constantly attacked the prosecutor, the process, and even the House Judiciary Committee chairman, Henry Hyde, rather than trying to ascertain the facts of the President's actions. In other words, she either did not understand the purpose for which she was there, or she had her own particular agenda.

The purpose of the committee hearing was to ascertain

whether President Clinton should be impeached based upon the evidence presented by the Independent Counsel and the Judiciary Committee members. If the facts were not there, Clinton would not have been impeached.

Some may disagree. Some may think that all the Republicans were biased. But we cannot deny that the purpose of the impeachment hearing was to determine whether the House should forward to the Senate for trial, articles of impeachment against President Clinton.

Similarly, in the Senate, the bombastic rhetoric by the White House counselors was designed to discredit the Starr Report, the House Managers and the process in general. The rhetoric was not only misleading, it was dishonest! The purpose of the trial was to get to the truth, not to parse words, split legal hairs, or denounce the constitutionality of the process.

We may argue all we want about the merits of the case for or against the results of the impeachment and the trial, but we cannot escape the fact that the rhetoric, particularly from the Democratic side of the aisle, was clearly not focused on the issues presented by the Judiciary Committee. Often the debate was not focused on the allegations or on trying to uncover the truth. Often rhetoric was used to try to steer the debate to other issues, including supporting the notion that President Clinton was actually a victim.

The debate was clearly about politics. It was not about searching for the truth.

Why would the Republican House Managers put their careers on the line in attempting to oust the President from office if they knew in advance that they would not get 67 Senators to vote in favor of conviction? Perhaps, just perhaps, they were actually convinced of the President's guilt. Perhaps they were standing by their principles, no matter the cost to their careers!

Think about it. What was their purpose? What type

of person would put his job in jeopardy over an issue that cannot be won? If a person possesses integrity, he would. If a person believes that principles count, she would. If a person thinks that breaking the law and the disregard of the law have far reaching consequences to our nation's psyche and judicial system, he would.

Therefore, I contend that the Republican House Managers were truly convinced that they were right. They were willing to stand by their principles no matter the political dilemma in which they placed themselves. To think otherwise is to fail to understand the purpose of the impeachment hearing. I believe that the Republican House Managers were willing to sacrifice their political futures because they understood the consequences to this nation of disregarding the rule of law.

I also fully understand the purpose for which the White House counselors tried to defend the President. Their purpose, after declaring his behavior reprehensible and indefensible, was to attack the process, the prosecutor, and the motives of his political enemies. Theirs was quite the dilemma they established for themselves as they mounted one of the most unusual defenses of a client in the annals of American jurisprudence. How can anyone defend someone on the facts and the merits of the case after having just stated the behavior was indefensible?

Therefore it is interesting to ask, what was their real purpose? I believe their real purpose was to defend the President at all costs against conviction and removal simply because that's what the political reality dictated. There was no way that the Democrats could afford to lose to conservatives, no matter the merits of the Impeachment case.

Why else would they claim that the President did not perjure himself in the grand jury, that he did not obstruct justice, and then turn right around and claim that even if he did, this did not rise to the level of impeachable offenses.

He didn't lie or perjure himself, he only mislead! He didn't obstruct justice or tamper with witnesses; he only tried to refresh his memory! His behavior wasn't illegal; it was only reprehensible and indefensible!

What kind of defense is that?

And in the end, after the Senate trial was history, Judge Susan Webber Wright found the President in contempt of court for lying under oath—an oath he took freely to tell the truth, the whole truth and nothing but the truth! At least Judge Wright, of all the characters in this sordid soap opera, understood the purpose of the case before her, albeit her ruling was woefully late in coming.

This dishonest, hair splitting rhetoric galvanized both sides of the impeachment debate to the point that it caused many members of Congress, journalists and pundits alike to support their party affiliation and personal philosophy without regard to the truth or purpose behind the issue. Instead, they became a part of the incivility in the nation over this issue. That is why these highly partisan journalists, pundits, and members of Congress have added to the "ethical civil war" as described by Bill O'Reilly of the Fox News Channel O'Reilly Factor. Their dishonesty in trying to persuade the American public of the intent of one side or the other has contributed to this lack of civility. In other words, neither side trusts the other because each senses the dishonesty in the other's rhetoric.

Why is it so hard to tell the truth? Why do we have all these political machinations rather than an honest attempt to determine the truth?

My belief is that the Senators who argued passionately for dismissal of the charges or censure of the President, rather than conducting a full trial, did not understand the intent and purpose of an impeachment trial. This misunderstanding caused the Senate to fail to do its constitutional duty.

In the long run, after all is said and done and all the facts finally come out, history will vindicate the House for attempting to uphold the rule of law. The Senate will be forever tarnished for its failure to uphold the principles of right and wrong.

Let's talk a little bit now about a new form of political rhetoric that changed public discourse in the '90s.

Some place along the line we decided we wanted to avoid at any cost the possibility of offending anybody's sensibilities, so we became a nation of "Political Correctness". How did this happen? Just what is the purpose behind being PC?

The purpose, apparently, is to revise history. The PC Thought Police believe that by simply changing words, they are changing minds.

Not so!

For example, calling an American black man an African-American doesn't change a thing. If it did, then why not change my label to Scandinavian-American? Apparently, the thought is that if we don't comply with the demands of the politically correct in society regarding the naming of black Americans as African-Americans, or Filipinos as Asian-Americans, then we must be insensitive at least, or racist at best.

This notion, of course, is ridiculous. Should I be offended because I'm classified as a white American instead of a Scandinavian-American, a classification that better reflects my true heritage? Where is the offense? It doesn't make any sense.

Has this political correctness really changed my mind about black Americans in general because the PC crowd insists we refer to them as African-Americans? No. I still see them as Americans, only with dark skin. For all I know, they're not even from Africa. They may be from the Dominican Republic. More likely they are from New York, or Muncie.

And do we really think that I am so shallow a person that skin color or renaming themselves African-Americans is a greater issue to me than that of their character? Do we now think that my parents were racist because in their day they called the black man a Negro? Is that racist? I don't think so. To say otherwise is revising history in today's terms and today's language.

Martin Luther King said many years ago, "Judge my children by the content of their character, not by the color of their skin." With those true words in mind, I urge again that we reevaluate the purpose behind why we change words to suit the politically correct. Such changes represent a blatant attempt to revise history, and I have to wonder if it's a not so subtle attempt to get us all to think alike and feel guilty if we don't.

Defenders will tell us the purpose is to provide young black people, or any minority living in the United States, with a sense of pride for their heritage.

If that is the case, then call me a Scandinavian-American because I too need to sense pride in my heritage. But I do sense pride in my grandparents' heritage, even without reference to their native lands. My father's parents immigrated from Sweden and Finland, my mother's parents from Austria and Poland. But I'm an American and I'm proud of it. I defended my country in two wars and served proudly in the United States Navy. I did this as an American, not as a Scandinavian-American.

Renaming races by our ancestry only further divides us into separate classes of citizens based upon our skin color and ethnic background. Why can't we all just be proud to be called Americans?

But back to rhetoric.

Rhetoric is in fact defined as the persuasive use of language. It therefore follows that one must understand

and correctly use vocabulary words to be persuasive. It also follows that the misuse of vocabulary to make one's point either shows ignorance of the word and its meaning in that context, or it indicates a desire to be theatrical, dramatic or funny. There is a third alternative: it could reveal a motivation or intention to be deliberately deceptive.

Let me provide a few examples of words recently used in daily conversation by broadcasters, politicians, journalists and other celebrities that have taken the use of the English language to a new level. Some of these examples are just humorous and very harmless. Others convey dark images solely intended to manipulate, mislead or deceive the audience.

Congressman Charles Rangel is a Democrat from New York. While a guest on a Fox News Channel television show, he remarked about the Republican interpretation of the Constitution during the impeachment hearing as not only wrong, but also as "raping the Constitution."

Could he have used other less inflammatory words? Of course he could have. Why didn't he just say that in his opinion the Republicans have misinterpreted the Constitution? Well, that "sound bite" would have been less dramatic and would not have elicited the response that he intended. He intended, in my opinion, to persuade the viewers that the Republicans were mean spirited. He intended his connotation to mean exactly the same as "rape" implies—abusive treatment, deliberate violation. He wanted us to conjure up the most horrendous image and associate it with mean spirited Republicans. He wanted us to remember the most disgusting act perpetrated against women and associate that with mean spirited Republicans out to perpetrate a most disgusting act against the Constitution of the United States of America. It was an intentional misuse of the word in my opinion, only this time instead of being harmless it was misleading and deceitful.

Another classic example of a word deliberately misused for heightened effect concerns a television sports announcer during the 1999 Buick Open at Torrey Pines Golf Course in California. A not very well known professional golfer was tied with Tiger Woods at the 17th hole on the final day of the tournament. His tee shot landed amongst the trees to the left of the fairway, and he desperately needed to land his second shot on the green to remain in contention for the title. With great accuracy, he placed his shot between tree limbs and landed the ball firmly on the putting surface. The announcer described that perfect shot as very "courageous" under the circumstances because of the pressure on him to compete with the famous Tiger Woods.

Oh really?

Courageous might be attempting a wedge shot from a sand trap in South Florida while dodging an alligator sunning himself on the hot sand. That's courageous, defined as the ability to face danger without fear. A golf shot from amongst the trees (with no alligators in sight) is hardly courageous. That illustration may not seem very important, and of course it is harmless, but it is an example of the misuse of language that confuses people. I know that most golf aficionados understood what the announcer meant by that comment. But to use the word "courageous" in that context demeans its true meaning. After seeing men die bravely in combat, I'm sensitive to the misuse of powerful words like "courage."

Another example is from a New York Post column written by David Gelernter. He describes George W. Bush's "compassionate conservatism" as "...allowing moderate Republicans to be seduced by the language of liberalism, merely because they don't want the Cultural Establishment to hate them."

In other words, what the phrase implies is that other

conservatives are not compassionate. Of course that's not true, but words do have meaning. This type of language once again plays into the liberal thinking that Republicans, especially conservative Republicans, are mean spirited because allegedly only a few of them are compassionate. The phrase sticks, and moderate Republicans slip easily into the trap.

Recently Governor Jesse Ventura of Minnesota apologized for his tongue-in-cheek comment on the David Letterman Show for saying that St. Paul, the twin-city to Minneapolis where he grew up, must have had their city streets designed by drunken Irishmen. Now to most observers this was funny—after all it was uttered on a late-night comedy show. But the elders on the city council of St. Paul felt compelled to pass a city resolution that said the streets were designed that way "to keep wrestlers and other undesirables out."

Was the city council trying to be cute? Did they think they were being funny too? You decide. But one comment was uttered in jest on a comedy show. The resolution in response was passed by a city council (which some may claim is also a comedy show) in the hallowed halls of city government.

To understand this farce, we must look at the motive, the intent of the utterance. Governor Ventura's comment, to most observers, was made in jest. Those who saw the show on television and could actually see his "body" language knew it was just a joke. The city council obviously had no sense of humor and responded with a lack of civility. Governor Ventura's intent was to be funny. The city council's purpose was to get even.

A more sinister lack of civility occurred on the Conan O'Brien Show with guest Alec Baldwin, the liberal activist who fancies himself important politically. He went into a rage over Congressman Henry Hyde's stance during President Clinton's impeachment trial and rallied the audience (and the viewers) to go down to Hyde's house and "kill" his wife and children. Sure, this was tongue-in-cheek humor on a late night comedy show. But there are plenty of kooks and ideologues that might think that Alec Baldwin was serious (and not acting) about his passionate hatred for Henry Hyde.

Was this rhetoric necessary? Do you find a difference in motive behind the remarks made by Governor Ventura and those made by Alec Baldwin? I think there is a big difference in motive. Was the motive humor, or was the motive anger? What was the real purpose behind their comments? I believe you will conclude that there was clearly a big difference in motive, and therefore intent, behind their comments.

And if it is considered funny to jest about killing Henry Hyde and his family for his actions during the impeachment trial, then consider this. Doug Tracht was a radio shock-jock known as "the Greaseman" on Classic Rock 94.7 WARW-FM in Washington, D.C. He commented on Grammy-winning black hip-hop artist Lauryn Hill's new hit song in this fashion: "No wonder people drag them behind trucks," he said, referring to the Jasper, Texas murder of James Byrd, Jr., a black man who was chained and dragged behind a pickup truck until he was beheaded. Radio station authorities appropriately fired "the Greaseman" for his insensitive racist comments.

But why was he fired? Was he advocating violence against blacks? Was he crudely showing intolerance? Or was he trying to be humorous?

The station claims he was fired because of his "trivialization of an unspeakable act of violence now at the heart of the national debate on race." I agree. I see it as not only a racist remark made against a black entertainer, but also as a disregard for the life of a black man so brutally murdered. It was dangerous commentary. It was unwarranted, uncivil, and clearly not funny.

However, let's back up a moment.

If we agree that "the Greaseman" was implying that violence against black people was okay, then you must also ascribe to a similar point of view regarding Alec Baldwin's remark on the Conan O'Brien Show about violence against Henry Hyde and his family. Alec Baldwin's remarks may not have been racist, but they were implying to some that violence was okay.

Why didn't the officials in charge of the Conan O'Brien Show, or the network executives, at least condemn Alec Baldwin's actions? Their silence invites more troubling questions.

Do these two scenarios imply that we cannot ignore a comment if it is racist in tone, but we can ignore a comment about violence as long as it does not contain racist overtones? Or is it simply that we have been programmed for years to be totally outraged at the mere thought of a racist comment, but have become accustomed to the violent acts we see everyday on television?

I'm outraged that we need to make a distinction between the two. Advocating violence is advocating violence, no matter your race or gender. Violence alone should outrage everyone.

We have apparently become a people who possess "selective outrage," depending upon our personal moral views, philosophies of life, or agendas.

Disgusting rhetoric does not offend some. But I, for one, would like to see it curtailed on the public airways.

In my opinion, both Alec Baldwin and Doug Tracht intended to mislead their audiences while supporting their own personal agendas. If the authorities at WARW-FM in Washington, D.C., thought it serious enough to terminate "the Greaseman's" employment for advocating violence, then NBC ought to rethink its position and at least make a statement condemning Alec Baldwin's insensitive performance on the Conan O'Brien Show. At least, Doug Tracht has since apologized, whereas nothing was heard from Alec Baldwin, Conan O'Brien or the NBC executives.

We can not have it both ways. In my opinion, this type of invective was clearly not meant to be humorous, and it only adds to the incivility in our daily dialogues. What's incomprehensible is that one commentator got punished for his remark, and another who made a similar remark got nothing but applause. The purpose of their remarks was the same—to incite incivility if not outright violence—but the consequences were different. How fair is that?

It's really a shame that the din of public discourse today has so deadened our senses that we have developed what I call "selective outrage." It's equally a shame that we have "selective morals and ethics." And now, in this new PC climate, we have developed "selective reporting" and selective denunciation of outrageous comments and events.

We truly need to understand right from wrong and separate it from our liberal, moderate, conservative or political views.

Imagine if instead of Alec Baldwin, it had been Rush Limbaugh on the Conan O'Brien Show. Imagine further that those remarks were focused on Barney Frank, or Jesse Jackson, or Senator Barbara Boxer. Try to imagine the media outcry! The media would have labeled them homophobic, or racist, or sexist, respectively. Instead, the media was frightfully quiet, because Baldwin's remark fit neatly into its own political point of view, that Congressman Hyde was a worthy target of such violent commentary because of his unpopular (with the media) position on Impeachment. The media let its own political bias cloud its judgment of the purpose of Baldwin's words.

Another great example of the misuse of rhetoric is actor-producer Spike Lee's comments about NRA President Charlton Heston's endorsement of gun ownership. Isn't it a bit hypocritical to make films showing violence with handguns and then angrily denounce Heston for his stance? Indeed, Spike Lee's muddled comment about "...showing him (Heston)...with a .44 caliber bulldog..." appears to be advocating violence in the same vein as did Alec Baldwin. One must ask if there is any racial intent here. It certainly would have been labeled as such if the situation were reversed. The point, again, is that the remarks should be taken at face value (violence) and not analyzed in terms of whom they are directed towards.

I can't say it enough—advocating violence is advocating violence. Other factors may be involved, such as racism, or sexism, or political agendas, but the bottom line is that the *purpose* of the rhetoric in the above examples was the display of violence.

There are thousands of other examples we could cite amongst the personalities and celebrities who fill the airwaves and the newsprint today. Many people who believe passionately in a cause use these highly inflammatory words, out of context, to get their point across. But is it honest? A critical thinker can see right through their intentions. But, unfortunately, the average American all too often buys into the spin. This type of rhetoric exists everywhere—from our neighborhoods, to the city council, to the school boards around the nation.

It has to stop if we are going to bring back civility into our national dialogue.

We need to understand the meaning and context that our words convey when written or spoken. We need to reintroduce vocabulary to our adult population so that they can understand the meaning of the words they use. We need to ensure that we use them correctly in context.

We ought to start with such words as *principle, civility, values, rhetoric, oath, hypocrisy, ethics, morals, standards,* and *integrity.*

I wonder what percentage of the American population can successfully define the meaning of the above words? I believe that if we can not define their meaning, then of course it follows that we have no idea what its purpose is when they are uttered in an exchange of conversation or printed on a page.

"The Greaseman" would still be working at WARW-FM in Washington, D.C., if he had just been civil and thought about what he was about to say before he actually said it.

This is not rocket science!

"The trial of principle:
without it a man hardly knows
whether he is honest or not."
Henry Fielding
1701-1754

Chapter 4: The Purpose of Principles

The purpose of principles is to maintain steadfastly to a moral or ethical standard of right and wrong, no matter the situation or the consequences.

We've all heard of "situational ethics": I will abide by my principles of right and wrong, without regard to the consequences—except if it affects something dear to me or is not convenient at the moment. In other words, if absolutely necessary, I will purposely change my response to legitimate inquiries in order to protect my family from the police, to secure a promotion opportunity, or to gain approval of my loan application.

We are all confronted every day by moral and ethical decisions, both great and small. We may choose between greed and principle, or power versus responsibility, or obligations versus feelings, or fairness versus duty. We've all been there, some families more than others, and we've all made mistakes.

But the solution to these mistakes is to take responsibility for our actions and mend our ways. Most people do this, most of the time. Most people teach their children that to confess to a lie or admit to a wrong is the best course of action. Be man enough to admit your mistake, and don't compound the situation by further covering it up, we tell our children and remind ourselves.

And, above all, don't give in to "situational ethics." Be consistent. Steadfastly stand by your principles, regardless of the consequences.

Giving in to greed and to the lust for power, fame, or money for the wrong reasons—simply to get ahead—is not just a sin of the heart, it also truly reflects a lack of principles.

My father once made my twin brother and me return to a store and pay for some comic books we had stolen off the shelf. I'm not sure I was old enough to understand that I was in fact stealing them, but what I learned that day was not just that I had to pay for the merchandise, but also that I had to atone for my mistakes. My father insisted on this course of action even though he likely was embarrassed by his sons' actions. He could have taken the easy way out, giving us a good scolding but saying nothing to anyone else. Nobody saw us take the comics, and nobody was going to make us pay for them. But my father stood by his principles of right and wrong, and it made a lasting impression on me.

I have preached this to my children so much that I'm sure to this day they would without hesitation suggest one of my favorite sayings as an epitaph on my gravestone. Take your pick: "You can never undo what you've already done"; "Don't be sorry; be right"; "Stand by your principles, no matter the situation"; and, "What's its *purpose*?"

To demonstrate "situational ethics" to my son, I once

asked him what he would do at college if confronted by the campus police about his roommate's use of drugs. If the allegations were true, would he deny the accusation and cover for his roommate to avoid getting him into trouble? Or would he stand by his principles and tell the truth? My son got my message, but he wasn't comfortable with "ratting" on his friend. I told him a principled position would be to confront the situation well before the campus police arrived. He needed to tell his roommate that he didn't tolerate drug use, particularly in their dorm room. He needed to tell his friend emphatically that drug use was against the law, that it was wrong behavior.

"Situational ethics" is a tough call when someone close to you is involved in illegal behavior. But what about smoking in the restroom at work? That clearly isn't necessarily against the law in all places, but may violate company policy. Why not confront that behavior? Yet many of us are reluctant to confront this type of behavior unless we are a supervisor or in a position of authority. But why tolerate misbehavior at all? We need to understand that there was a reason for establishing a company policy about smoking in the building. There was a purpose behind the no smoking policy. If we understand the purpose—that the policy protects our health and safety—then we are free to act accordingly.

Let me give you a couple of examples in my life where principle won the day in my view, although the victories were not easy ones.

Earlier in my career, when I was a Commanding Officer of a helicopter squadron, I ran into harsh criticism from my chief petty officers, the senior enlisted managers and supervisors in my command. Almost all of them united against me because of the manner in which I was perceived to be giving special privileges to enlisted female members of my command over the males. The situation was this: most new members to an aviation squadron, particularly those in the aviation maintenance field, were assigned to the Line Division. This division washed aircraft, conducted routine preflight preparations, and did general servicing of aircraft for the day's flight schedule.

When I learned that some female sailors were pregnant, I directed that they be transferred to other less dangerous assignments, much to the consternation of my Chiefs. After weeks of hearing this grumbling, I finally called a meeting of the entire Chief Petty Officer Corps in the squadron to air our thoughts. Many Chiefs felt I was not being fair to the young males who, as a direct result of my new policy, ended up doing most of the dirty work in the squadron. However, when I explained that a pregnant woman might slip off the aircraft or inhale toxic aircraft cleansers to the detriment of her baby, I won over a few converts. But not all of them were convinced, and in fact, many were still angry at my decision. Some senior enlisted advisors and a few officers hinted that my action might lead to a slowdown of sorts to get my attention. However, I stuck to my principles because I did not want to make a decision that could have resulted in the termination of the life of the baby of one of my sailors.

Even to some of those skeptical chiefs, my answer wasn't good enough. (In my own view, no answer would have been good enough, because these few chiefs did not like women in the Navy in the first place, and by God, a sailor is a sailor is a sailor.) I could have easily given in to my middle managers to preserve the peace and ensure a one hundred percent effort on their part to get aircraft and detachments trained on time to go to sea, but I chose to do the right thing. I stuck by my principles. The chiefs were apparently convinced by the "Old Man's" attitude, as they maintained their professionalism and the grumblings soon ceased.

Another example occurred later in my career when I commanded a large amphibious assault ship in the Pacific. My boss—another Captain who was headquartered on my ship—and I did not see eye to eye on all situations, but I tried very hard to make that invisible to the crew.

However, it all came to a head in Thailand when my Supply Officer was ordered by my boss to provide monies from the ship's welfare and recreation fund to pay off local merchants in the city following our port visit. The Navy liaison officer stationed in Thailand wanted the Amphibious Task Group to pay local merchants prior to leaving for alleged damage or unpaid bills by the visiting Sailors and Marines.

The problem this order presented was twofold. First, welfare and recreation money was not the right purse to pay off what was little more than petty extortion; secondly, many of the ship's Sailors and Marines vehemently denied they owed bills. Some, if not most, of the allegations were a complete scam, and the local merchants had been doing this for years each time the American fleet departed. Fortunately for me, my Supply Officer had the utmost integrity and brought this to my attention. When I confronted my boss, he asked that I instead pay the money from the ship's operating funds. Again, this was illegal, even though it had been done this way in the past. My boss wanted to leave the port call with no outstanding bills, no fuss and no negative publicity for his command. I refused to comply.

Another Commanding Officer from another ship in the task group didn't see it as I did and provided the necessary monies from his ship's welfare and recreation fund. His ship's welfare and recreation fund was raided in the amount of close to $4,000 dollars, because he took the easy way out. The bottom line was his Sailors and

Marines were cheated.

Why did I go to all this fuss about money that didn't personally belong to me or to my Sailors and Marines? By not 'going along to get along,' all I did was upset my boss for no reason. But there was a good reason: it involved something called integrity and principle. When I was given the opportunity by Navy leadership to command, it was for the purpose of directing the efforts of my crew to train for combat and to use the resources given to us by the taxpayers to the best of my ability. It was not to be used, in my opinion, to ensure that I got promoted to the next rank, or to please the boss at the expense of the crew, or to be ranked number one of all the skippers in the task group. That incident did nothing to further my career, but it doesn't matter. It left me with my integrity!

In my opinion, I was the only one of four Captains who stood by his principles. I don't think the other three Captains ever felt guilt for their actions or lack of principles. One later retired after being discovered abusing the rules by illegally advancing enlisted members in his command while he was Commanding Officer of another ship. My boss never felt shame or ever apologized to me for trying to go around me directly to my Supply Officer. I wonder why he did that. Perhaps he knew in advance what my answer would be. But I know I did the right thing; I did not sacrifice my principles for a "good ticket" to promotion. In the end, I had a very successful Navy career, affirming my belief that integrity does count.

Principles are moral concepts grounded on a firm belief in a high standard of right and wrong. It follows that to understand the meaning of principle requires you to abide by a standard normally established by society. Also, one must be able to distinguish between what is right and wrong morally, legally and ethically. These notions are intertwined of course, but have distinctions. What may be legally right in the sense of legislation such as abortion is morally wrong in the sense of religious beliefs for many. What may be legally right and not criminal to professional businessmen and politicians may in fact be ethically wrong in the sense of violating a trust of proprietary knowledge.

My point is that principles should not be swayed on the basis of legislation making something legal, or policy making something inappropriate. Principles have to be grounded in a moral belief of right and wrong conduct.

The difficulty for many of us is to define our moral beliefs. It's much easier to understand and abide by written rules and regulations that strictly codify laws and policy. Violations of those written rules and regulations are clearly either illegal, unethical or both as the case may be, but violation of moral beliefs is normally a matter of conscience, rather than of crossing the line of codified rules.

The dilemma is particularly difficult if legislation and policy run counter to your moral beliefs. And I contend that we have from time to time codified some behavior mainly to counteract the moral outrage that stems from the behavior in question. For example, why did we codify abortion? Perhaps because those people who lack morals need legal cover to defend their immoral actions. It is much easier to explain that they are simply following the law than to answer critics who note that abortion takes an innocent life.

Once again, we need to understand the purpose in legalizing immoral behavior.

Many Americans find it very difficult to follow established rules and regulations, particularly if they disagree with their purpose. However, we establish rules and regulations for the common good, and we expect citizens to obey them. But if there is a lack of enforcement or even worse, a lack of caring, should we simply disregard those rules and regulations knowing full well that we will probably never suffer any of the consequences associated with the violation? Of course not! Whether we get caught or not for violating an established rule or regulation is not the issue. The issue is to stand steadfastly by a moral or ethical standard of right and wrong behavior regardless of the situation or the consequences. That's known as having principles. Some of us truly believe in standing by our principles; others like President Clinton appear to have no shame, only rage at getting caught. Still others, like many of the members of the International Olympic Committee, have fallen prey to greed, power and perks. This is particularly disturbing coming from an organization that formerly espoused the ideals of principles.

Remember, intentionally violating an established company or societal standard is to violate one's own principles of right and wrong. If we tell ourselves or others that we had a reason for violating the standard, then we are engaging in situational ethics.

*"Discipline is the soul of
an army. It makes small
numbers formidable; procures
success to the weak, and
esteem to all."*
George Washington
1732 - 1799

Chapter 5: The
Purpose of Discipline

**The purpose of discipline is to elicit a specified
and predictable pattern of behavior.**

Just as with standards, discipline is a fundamental
aspect of civilized society. Discipline is probably most
notable in the military, but it also exists in athletic
programs, the police force, fire departments, the National
Guard, schools, clubs, and associations. It is also a defining
characteristic of stable, successfully functioning families.

Discipline is normally associated with training or a
learning environment. Belonging to an organization or an
activity that conducts training for the purpose of
establishing a certain pattern of behavior or character
demands discipline that is intended to ensure that specified
values are passed along to all members of the organization.
Different organizations may have different values, but their

purpose of discipline is the same.

I contend that without discipline and its enforcement, those values lose their significance.

For example, discipline in the military, particularly for soldiers, is designed to elicit immediate obedience to orders, which will improve teamwork and ensure trust among its members. The goal is to establish an effective fighting force determined to win the objective. A military unit cannot win its objective if it lacks the trust of its members; soldiers will hesitate to do their duty and many will die in the subsequent confusion.

Similarly, sports teams require discipline to ensure they work as a team. Their goal is to win the game. If this goal is to be achieved, the defense and the offense must play equally well. The purpose of discipline is designed to guarantee that everyone plays by the same rules for the common good. If all participate at the same level of effort, they all can expect the same level of achievement. That level may not necessarily win the objective or win the game, but the effort exhibited by all its members, knowing that they played by the rules, that they worked as hard as they could, invokes pride and trust in one another. Theirs is a winning attitude. They showed purpose in their endeavor.

The above examples demonstrate that discipline is the necessary ingredient to foster a winning combination. Of course, there is a difference in the intensity of discipline applied by military drill instructors as compared with the discipline applied by high school football coaches, but their purpose is the same. If effective, discipline produces the desired result. Show me a military unit or a sports team which does not have a healthy dose of discipline, and I'll show you a group of individuals—not a team—who do not possess either the level of teamwork, morale or trust among its members to achieve its intended goal.

Discipline can go beyond the normal meaning of training designed to elicit a certain kind of behavior. It can also mean a condition of order based upon obedience to authority. This is actually the more common definition in use today. It exists among families, churches, businesses, schools, governments, and associations. Each group has its own particular set of rules and regulations that they desire their associates to follow. These regulations vary from dress codes for work or school, curfew hours for children, facial hair policies for men, who can partake of communion, and any other number of policies designed to establish the values each group desires to have followed in order for its reputation to be projected in a desired manner.

Obedience to rules and regulations requires training (discipline), and effective enforcement of those rules and regulations ensures compliance.

There are many individuals in society who disregard rules and regulations and the law, and then claim persecution to management or even to the courts when they are confronted for violating them. These people have either forgotten the rules governing their employment, refused to obey the law because they don't like its restrictions, or have simply neglected to comply with them for their own selfish reasons.

Not agreeing with rules does not allow you the privilege of disregarding them. If you don't like them, change them. We live in a democracy. Exercise your powers and rights. Get the union to help sway management. Have the city council amend the legislation. But don't whine because you were caught violating them.

Families have a different problem. Most families don't have formal rules and regulations posted on the refrigerator door, but they do have informal policies that parents expect their children to follow. Violation of these rules normally places some kind of restriction on the children, perhaps being "grounded." Kids don't like rules, but most understand the consequences, if they have been properly educated as to the concept of right and wrong.

When society does not establish rules to govern standards of behavior, people become uncivil towards one another. Even worse, when society does not enforce the rules, citizens become numb to their meaning. That's why an outcry is often heard from motorists who get stopped for speeding or rolling through a stop sign. They are incensed that a policeman is not out catching "bad guys" but are instead issuing them a citation. These complainers do not understand the purpose of the laws governing their behavior while driving a motor vehicle. I'm not suggesting we all become Mr. and Mrs. Goody-Two-Shoes, but I am suggesting that we need to reevaluate the purpose for which the policeman has pulled us over in the first place. If we don't like the posted speed limit, think it is too slow for the conditions, then we should lobby our city councilman to get it changed. Why complain when the police officer is simply doing his duty? What we are really asking the officer to do is to be "selective" in the laws he or she is to enforce.

The citation may seem unfair, but the blame for the situation does not belong to the police officer.

Enforcement of laws or regulations is the cornerstone in ensuring that discipline is maintained. We cannot have discipline without enforcement. Moreover, lack of enforcement leads to the inevitable complaint of unfairness when it is randomly applied. It sends the wrong message to those who choose to disobey and to those who are looking for a standard to follow.

Youngsters are particularly impressionable. They

watch and listen and learn from their elders and peers. If they assume everybody breaks certain rules and regulations, they may wrongly conclude that those rules don't apply to them.

That's why enforcement of rules and regulations is so important. If everybody plays by the rules, everybody understands the expectations and the consequences. It is as simple as that! In other words, let's understand the purpose and necessity of discipline in our society. To ignore it is to deny the truth.

Why are we so incensed with authority figures, particularly when we have violated the law? Or violated the company smoking policy? Do we consider some laws or policies more important than others, and therefore disregard what we deem as minor offenses as being simply irrelevant? If so, then haven't we become judgmental for the wrong reasons? What gives us the right to determine which laws we should obey? Or which company policies we should follow and which ones we should disregard?

I believe our society is drifting again today (much as in the days of the "Wild West") towards becoming highly individualistic. Many of us simply do not accept authority figures telling us what to do and regulating our lives. This is especially true when we have judged in our own mind that some rules or regulations are silly and unimportant. What's the big deal rolling through a stop sign if it is clear and I don't hit anybody? Why can't I smoke in the restroom if nobody is around, instead of smoking outside?

But that's not how democracy works.

As individuals, we do not have the authority to change rules, regulations and the motor vehicle laws on the spot. Think of the turmoil if city councils approved rolling stops. There would be no purpose behind it except for personal convenience by those people who think road safety is unimportant. It would be a disaster. If we changed the rules to suit ourselves, we would no longer have a democracy, we would have anarchy.

But worse than a lack of discipline and a lack of enforcement, is the lack of community outrage for violation of rules and regulations. When is the last time you told your co-worker not to smoke in the restroom? Or honked your horn at the teenager who recklessly cut you off because he didn't stop at the corner? There may be good reason not to confront these people, but by avoiding confrontation we've actually enabled their behavior. We've shown our indifference to the situation.

So why do we react so passively when we know our inaction goes against our own interests, not to mention against the interests of the larger society as a whole?

I believe the answer is not very complex. The social culture in our society today says we cannot be judgmental, and therefore we cannot or will not confront right from wrong. We refuse to get involved, under the misguided notion that when someone is doing something harmful, it is their own business.

The '90s cultural wars with their breeding grounds in liberal college curriculums, coupled with the lax discipline children receive at school and at home today, have taught us that certain rules and regulations have a bias of racial or ethnic overtones. Advertising has told us to "do your own thing." Movies and television have shown us "in your face" attitudes. Sitcoms denigrate authority figures. People of faith are proclaimed to be right wing fanatics. Audiences salivate over outlandish behavior observed on The Jerry Springer Show. All of these influences have permeated the American psyche.

The more outrageous the better. It's cool! And when caught, the common response is to complain that everybody does it, rather than admitting to the wrong.

Police officers have been painted with a broad brush as racist, and denigrated for enforcing laws designed to protect us all. The military has been described as warmongers by the liberal left when ordered by competent authority to do their duty. Defense attorneys have labeled district attorneys and prosecutors as overly aggressive, simply for defending the rule of law during civil or criminal cases against their clients.

Of course there are bad cops and misguided soldiers and deceitful lawyers, but trying to portray authority figures as the "bad guys" is patently absurd, not to mention, counter productive. Discipline and enforcement of standards is a necessary ingredient to maintaining law and order, otherwise chaos rules the day.

Why are we so afraid to enforce the rules and regulations already on the books? We don't need new "hate crimes" law, we simply need to enforce the existing laws pertaining to violence. Why do we insist on legislating against hate (an emotion), rather than against violence (an act)? It shouldn't matter what the motive is as long as the perpetrator is arrested and tried—violence is violence. I don't believe that there is overwhelming evidence which supports the need to write a "hate crimes" law under the assumption jurisdictions are not arresting those involved for violent crimes. If that evidence exists, go to the source: fire the district attorney, or the sheriff, don't write new laws.

Do we really need to federalize every crime because of the brutality of violence against homosexuals, or women, or blacks, or even police officers. Of course not. This outcry is little more than an emotional outburst by certain groups in our society. For fear of being called a homophobe or a racist or some other name, we pass laws to make us "feel" better.

Think about it! What is the purpose for providing a

federal "hate crimes" law that can't be served by enforcing existing law in every state?

It reminds me of the attempt by feminists to pass the Equal Rights Amendment to ensure "equal rights" for women. Isn't that already guaranteed by the Constitution?

Let's just equally enforce and respect the laws we already have!

*"Man must cease
attributing his problems to
his environment, and learn
again to exercise his will—
his personal responsibility
in the realm of faith and
morals."*
Albert Schweitzer

Chapter 6: The Purpose of Responsibility

**The purpose of responsibility is to account for
one's actions; to impart a duty or obligation.**

Most unbiased Americans, if you believe the polls,
can properly understand that the military and economic
situation that has caused the Iraqi people so much pain
and suffering, is the result of the governmental policies of
President Saddam Hussein. They hold him responsible
for his own actions during the 1990 takeover of Kuwait
and his subsequent violation of the agreement to abide by
the terms of the United Nations Resolutions following the
removal of his armies from Kuwait. Why then, did so many
people not hold President Clinton responsible for his
actions which caused his impeachment and trial by the
United States Congress? It's a dichotomy of tremendous
magnitude that I do not understand.

It clearly follows, whether you like or dislike Saddam Hussein or Bill Clinton, that their personal actions and theirs alone, caused their predicaments. Saddam Hussein has never accepted responsibility for his actions in invading the sovereign nation of Kuwait, despite his protests that Kuwait was simply a runaway province of Iraq. Even now he continues to deny responsibility for his actions in defying the United Nations' sanctions imposed upon him after his armies ouster from Kuwait.

Similarly, Bill Clinton never accepted personal responsibility for putting the nation through an impeachment trial, despite the fact that he was impeached and fifty Senators found him guilty of obstruction of justice.

Bill Clinton's personal misbehavior in and out of the Oval Office led him to be accused of obstruction of justice and perjury before the grand jury, after solemnly taking an oath to tell the truth, the whole truth, and nothing but the truth. Although not removed from office, half of the Senators still found him guilty of those charges.

His narrow escape from the consequences of his actions came down to a political decision, not a legal one. To think otherwise is simply to deny the facts.

I still believe that the President should have resigned or been removed from office because he committed crimes for which other citizens go to jail. However, it was not up to me, nor was it up to any other journalist, pundit, political commentator, or public opinion poll to decide that fate.

The Constitution left that decision to the United States Senate. Those one hundred Senators who took an oath of impartiality needed to independently determine by their own conscience, not clouded by politics or the polls, whether Bill Clinton should have been removed from office.

If I had been one of those one hundred members of the jury, I would have asked myself these two questions. What were the motives behind his actions? Wasn't he responsible and ultimately accountable for the charges against him?

I believe he was responsible for his own actions and should have been held accountable for them. If you accept that notion, no other consequence other than removal was acceptable. Clinton's type of behavior certainly would not have been tolerated in my office or my household, and I doubt any Senator would accept this type of behavior in his or her home or office.

The argument that you cannot overturn a popular election of the President of the United States through the impeachment process would have had some merit if the Framers had not included the impeachment clause in the Constitution. Just as the Constitution includes a process for popularly electing the Head of State, it also includes a removal process, known as Impeachment.

Although the President was not removed from office, many Democrats wanted to express their outrage at his behavior through a vote of censure. So what happened to that Resolution of Censure so loudly proclaimed by Senator Diane Feinstein and others, who assured it would be forthcoming after the Senate returned from recess? How did their outrage dissipate so fast? Didn't they still feel it was their responsibility to censure the President for his misbehavior since they didn't remove him from office? Or was this just another one of those "selective outrages" without "teeth" to demonstrate their concern and get on the public record? And why hasn't the press inquired into this hypocrisy? Just why did the press drop this whole issue with hardly a murmur since?

Mrs. Clinton was widely praised for defending her husband. "Standing by her man" was viewed as honorable, and I would accept that view if I were convinced that she was unaware of her husband's sexual exploits and his later denials under oath during the depositions and his grand jury appearance. But I don't accept that she did not know. I do accept that it was very convenient for her to appear not to know the details. Especially when she was interviewed on national television and defended her husband against the charges of lying under oath and obstruction of justice. In that same interview she acknowledged that violating the sanctity of the oath was a serious matter. Therefore, should I give her the benefit of the doubt at the time? Perhaps!

But what about today, after the facts are known? Today she is fully aware of her husband's actions and denials. Should she still get a pass for defending the indefensible? Can she still be regarded as honorable for defending her husband now that she knows that he lied under oath? Mrs. Clinton cannot have it both ways.

She was either duped by her husband and defended him, later to learn the truth; or she deceived the public, defended her husband and later the truth came out. But either way, she made a stance on national television for the sanctity of the oath, and she ought to be held accountable for her actions. Does she still defend her husband's actions? I haven't yet heard a reporter question her stance. I don't think she was honorable, I think she lacked principles because of the stakes involved in remaining in office with all the perquisites she now enjoys.

When asked a question about President Clinton's personal behavior, the overwhelming response by his defenders in and out of Congress was that the President's behavior was reprehensible and indefensible. If it was indefensible, why did they defend him?

I believe they defended him because the President's lawyers, with help from the media, successfully labeled the President as a victim, and the poll numbers supported that theory. The White House spin machine rightly guessed that if the President could be portrayed as a victim of an out of control prosecutor, or a grand right-wing conspiracy, or a young stalker, then they need not defend his actions. Instead, they could concentrate on destroying the integrity of the process and the public image of the women making the allegations.

Thus Paula Jones, Kathleen Willey and Monica Lewinsky were depicted as after the President for their own personal reasons: money, fame or both.

It's very interesting to find out months after the impeachment trial that a federal judge determined that President Clinton lied under oath in the Paula Jones deposition. Although he escaped removal from office, after the fact he was held in contempt of court. We've also found out since then that Kathleen Willey passed a FBI polygraph test about the events she claims happened to her in the White House. And, of course, after seven months of strenuous denials, the events about Monica Lewinsky's sexual exploits with the President finally emerged as truth, even down to the lurid story about the stained dress.

What was the media's responsibility in this situation? Shouldn't they have also questioned the motives of the President's defenders as well as the motives of the women?

My own feeling is that if the press, as well as the Senate's prosecutors, had personalized their questions, the result would have turned out dramatically different. For example, what if Monica Lewinsky was your daughter, how would you feel about removing the President from office?

What if Kathleen Willey were your sister, how would you feel about removing the President from office? What if Paula Jones were your wife and she was denied her day in court, would you favor removing the President from office?

Viewed this way, events take on greater significance when one is personally involved.

Most people disregard outcomes of trials unless the trial personally affects them or their loved ones. They tend to side with the perceived victim. That's why juries of late have sided with plaintiffs on huge monetary settlements against big corporations.

Regardless of the merits of the case, they see the plaintiff as a victim of those big companies with no heart and plenty of purse strings. Often they support defendants if they suspect police brutality or simply the claim of it by their attorneys. They side with human emotion, faults and frailties versus an uncaring institution bound by policy and the rule of law. They label prosecutors out of control for using standard procedures while investigating their cases. In a strange sense, justice in America today is all about "winning" as opposed to "seeking the truth."

I am convinced that any Senator who was personally involved in this sordid escapade by the White House, or truly believed in "seeking the truth" as opposed to "winning" the case for their side, would have voted for conviction.

During the next town hall meeting conducted by one of your congressional representatives or Senators, ask him or her the above questions, and see whether they would have voted for conviction if they were personally involved. Ask them if they would have resigned under similar circumstances. Or if in fact, they would now vote to retain Senator Bob Packwood of Oregon for his sexual misconduct while in office, which in my mind did not come close to the magnitude of sexual misbehavior conducted by the President.

There really is only one answer they can give. Any other response is simply dishonest. Invoking the notion that the President should not be removed from office because it takes a higher standard to remove a popularly elected President, is a smokescreen. As almost every Senator acknowledged, the type of behavior displayed by the President was reprehensible, some said impeachable, and clearly would not have been tolerated in most households. In fact, the proposed censure resolution used similar words to describe perjury and obstruction of justice;

the only difference between censure and conviction was removal from office.

Can we be as brutally honest in our assessment of his behavior? Do we condone what he did because the economy is good? Or don't we care because we were not personally involved.

My guess is that if we were personally involved by being a family member or friend of one of the women involved in the President's misbehavior, we would clearly see the injustice.

Now that our President has thoroughly trashed the concept of personal responsibility, how do we reclaim it? How do we reclaim the virtue of accepting responsibility and accountability for our actions and our words?

First, we must redefine right from wrong. Ideally, our conscience should be speaking to us loudly and clearly and without hesitation. The difference between right and wrong behavior should be as ingrained in our thought processes as memorizing our multiplication tables or reciting the alphabet.

But it is not that easy.

It is easy to define murder, rape, incest, and theft as wrongful behavior, because one party is clearly a victim. But what about adultery, abortion, off color jokes, and swearing—are these also considered wrong behaviors? Adultery, to many, is consensual and therefore not wrong. Abortion is legal, take a look at Roe vs Wade. We all tell jokes, some people are just too sensitive. Bad language is everywhere in the movies, television, books. So don't be a prude, we tell ourselves.

Rather than justifying support for our position based upon a common excuse, we need to relearn that behavior, intentionally or unintentionally, which can cause mental, physical or emotional hurt, is bad behavior. Therefore, lying, cheating and incivility are just as wrong as any other behavior which disrespects another person's rights. Just remember, it's as simple as the Biblical phrase "do unto others as you would have them do unto you."

But beyond recognizing right and wrong behavior, how do we hold responsible people accountable?

We need to enforce existing laws, bureaucratic regulations, company policies and parental rights. We need to insist on civility to one another. We need to loudly protest our displeasure with uncivil behavior. We need to defend our parental rights over what our children should see and hear. And we need to hold accountable executives and other officials in charge who do not uphold decent standards. We must fire or reprimand those responsible for inappropriate and wrong behavior.

Charlton Heston, in a February 1999 speech entitled "Winning the Cultural War," given before the Harvard Law School Forum, talked about public disobedience when confronted with unacceptable "politically correct" behavior. He opined that the politically correct crowd in the liberal-leaning corridors of academia has taught us what to think in the classrooms and what to say in the politically correct world. Next, he suggested, these same people would tell us what actions to take.

He challenged the students to be the vanguards for free thought and to stand up in nonviolent disobedience, as Dr. Martin Luther King, Jr. did so many years ago.

In other words, he was advocating critical thinking. He was urging them to challenge immoral and unacceptable behavior by peacefully demonstrating before school boards, advertisers, executives and boards of directors, to hold them accountable for their actions.

Unless we suddenly see resurgence in the concept of morality among the American populace, the only way to win the cultural war in society is to protest loudly and politely disobey unacceptable behavior.

Get involved! Understand the *purpose* of responsibility in winning the war against "political correctness."

*"God will not take you to
task for vain words in your
oaths, but He will take you to
task for what your hearts
have amassed."*
The Koran

Chapter 7: The Purpose of an Oath

*The purpose of an oath is to take a solemn promise
or declaration before God, to committing yourself to
upholding the ideals of an office, marriage, institution
or association to the best of your ability.*

Many people in public life take an oath of office.
Federal, state and city officials take an oath to their duties.
Officers and enlisted members of the armed forces take
an oath of allegiance to defend the Constitution of the
United States of America against all enemies foreign and
domestic. Civic groups and Scouts take an oath to be
faithful to their group. Doctors take a Hippocratic Oath.
Juries take an oath of impartiality, as did the Senators
during the Clinton Impeachment trial. And, of course,
William Jefferson Clinton took an oath when he accepted

his responsibility as President of the United States.

Even ordinary citizens take a vow of marriage. It is quite common amongst the American population to be familiar with oaths and vows and pledges.

In my childhood, we learned the Pledge of Allegiance to the United States of America. I wonder how many children today can recite that pledge.

I wonder even more how many Americans understand the purpose of that pledge, or the purpose of any vow or oath they take. Does the average American citizen really understand what it means to commit to an oath or pledge?

This raises questions: should I feel embarrassment if I don't live up to that oath; and if I don't live up to that oath should I resign or be removed from my position?

You will find that more and more people today simply disregard the virtues that bind us to commitment. They think it is their right not to conform, yet still to be included. They think that their individualism allows them to behave the way they want to without regard to consequences or to the oath that they voluntarily took. In other words, they do not understand the *purpose* behind their oath.

Our society has almost come to the point where we are guaranteed a right "not" to be held accountable to our commitments or our contracts. We have given up on trying to enforce established standards in the form of oaths, vows and pledges. A promise today means I will try rather than I will comply. And if I don't comply, "Please don't hold me accountable, because after all I am only a human being with many faults."

This is the reasoning behind many people's acceptance of President Clinton's misbehavior. He is not a saint, but rather a human being with faults. Forget the oath he took to faithfully enforce the laws of the land. He tried. The same can be said of the Senators who spoke out about their views of the impeachment of President Clinton before the trial was over and all the facts were presented. What happened to their oath of impartiality?

"I'm more than a juror; I'm also a judge," said Senator Harkin. "Therefore, that excuses my behavior and allows me to speak out regardless of whether I took an oath to be impartial. In any case, it doesn't matter; the people in my district want me to vote this way anyway," he must have been thinking.

The same can be said of former Speaker of the House of Representatives Newt Gingrich. He voluntarily took an oath of office, not only as a Congressman, but also as the Speaker to uphold the honor of his office. He let us down with his failure to be fully honest with those investigating his political activities and fund-raising efforts, and he was fined appropriately.

Newt Gingrich is not alone among politicians, however. There are many that violate the true spirit of the oath of their office to support their own personal agendas and to ensure they continue to receive the support of their constituents, regardless of principle involved.

Many elected and appointed officials in government are susceptible to violating their oaths simply because they get caught in a dilemma deciding between principle and purpose on the one hand, and power and prestige on the other. Retired Lieutenant Colonel Oliver North, USMC, former National Security advisor in the Reagan-Bush White House fell into this trap. Although he was viewed as a hero in the Congressional hearings into the Iran-Contra affair, I believe he violated his oath as an officer in the United States Marine Corps while assigned to the staff of the National Security Council. He was willing to deceive the nation, while not fully telling the truth about the events surrounding the Iran-Contra affair.

The power, prestige and perquisites of the White House diluted his judgment, because he chose power over principle. It was his obligation to ensure that he maintained the highest integrity in conjunction with his assignment. And for those who supported Ollie North, because he was simply following the orders given by his superiors, I say there was a better alternative: North could have resigned his position and asked for a transfer. But he didn't want to give up a choice assignment that most military officers never see. It's a tough decision to make, but one that should have been made.

What about marriage vows? This vow, often before God, is no longer sacred to many people. So what if I cheat on my spouse? Apparently many people believe most people do cheat. We have accepted the notion that oaths, vows and pledges don't really mean we must behave the way the oath or vow or pledge demands us to behave. We have looked the other way, believing that most oaths and vows are unenforceable over time anyway. We lack the inner courage even to display our indignation with those who disregard their pledges or marriage vows.

Years ago, most of us took seriously our oaths of office and our vows of marriage. We considered swearing our oath before God, with our right hand in the air and our left hand on the Bible, making a sacred commitment to do our very best. We were embarrassed or shamed if we failed to uphold our commitments, and we resigned our offices or positions because of that shame. It was only the "bad elements" of society who disregarded their oaths after so swearing. Today that shame reaches into the highest levels of society and government, including the White House.

The difference, however, between today and an earlier era, is that now not everyone feels shame for their failure to fulfill their commitment. Today, instead of feeling shame, we make excuses for our failures. "It's not my fault!" "My father was an abusive alcoholic!" "My people have been repressed for years by government policies!" "I'm only human!"

Once we extolled the virtues of principles and integrity, and pledged before God our sacred commitment to do our jobs to the very best of our abilities. Today we "affirm" (versus "swear to") our commitments. This subtle change has allowed us to feel less guilty if we fail, because we no longer have God as our witness. We no longer have to feel shame before God that we have broken our commitment to our duties. In fact, we have evolved so far in our thinking that by today's definition, we no longer consider a promise, a pledge. A promise is not sworn before God, it is merely my word. And my word is only as good as the circumstances that surround it. If the situation changes, I am entitled to back away from that earlier promise.

Look at what is happening in the professional sports world. A long-term contract isn't worth even the price of the paper it is written on anymore, because as soon as one athlete renegotiates a higher salary, another athlete with equal ability demands equal compensation, regardless of the terms of his previous contract. Demands to renegotiate contracts are rationalized because the circumstances have changed. In other words, contracts signed and sealed by the player and the team are invalidated at will, regardless of their signatures. What does that say about the value of contracts? Why do we let this happen? Is it the threat that the athlete will sit out the year rather than suffer the indignity of playing for only $4 million a year versus $5 million? This is obscene, yet the sports world hardly blinks an eye as it happens over and over again.

This evolution of disregard for sacred commitments has completely denigrated the true meaning of solemnly taking an oath. An oath no longer has the fear associated with the wrath of God coming down upon those of us who fail to live up to our commitments. This has caused us to continue down that slippery slope where promises are broken without shame or remorse. In fact, it has caused us to falsely promise (lie about) something, when we know full well that we never intend to fulfill it. It has affected how we deal with one another and with our contractual obligations to each other, knowing that a promise is simply a statement of an attempt to do something rather than an honest commitment to comply with it. The resulting lack of purpose to fulfill our word (promise) or our deed (contractual obligations) is not uncommon. We don't feel guilt or shame or remorse for our failures; we simply rationalize our behavior with excuses.

This disregard for our sacred commitments has had a deleterious affect on the American psyche that goes well beyond the simple act of failing to honor a pledge or a vow or an oath of office. Such failures have become so routine that they are almost acceptable behavior, further adding to our distrust and incivility towards one another.

Some institutions, however, are fighting hard to maintain their values and the meanings of their oaths. The Boy Scouts of America is a good example. They believe in God, and they don't condone homosexuality. They are standing by their principles (and oaths) to fight forced inclusion of beliefs they do not consider part of the value system central to their organization. They are fighting and winning in the courts for what they believe is right. Why should the American Civil Liberties Union try to impose on a private organization like the Boy Scouts of America their belief that a homosexual police officer has the right to be reinstated as a Boy Scout leader? Whose civil liberties are they trying to protect, the homosexual police officer, or the impressionable young boys? And why is the ACLU involved in trying to force the courts to reinstate twin boys, who have declared themselves atheists and who refuse to recite the Boy Scout Oath because it contains the word God? The ACLU needs to reexamine its purpose in trying to impose its beliefs on a private organization. The point is really very simple in my opinion. The Boy Scouts of America and any other private organization are fully within their rights to hire and fire whomever they like according to their rules, regulations and values. It is clearly their right, and theirs alone, to change their organization as they see fit.

Oaths, pledges and vows are all about commitment to an ideal. A military officer commits himself to an oath to support and defend the Constitution of the United States of America against all enemies, foreign and domestic. An American citizen commits himself to a Pledge of Allegiance to the flag of the United States of America and to the Republic for which it stands. A husband and wife commit themselves to a marriage before God "...for better or for worse, in good times and bad..." All of these ideals—the Constitution, the American flag and the institution of marriage before God—are special commitments that require extraordinary fortitude, hard work and dedication. Special commitments demand special loyalty above and beyond an ordinary commitment. That's why we require an oath, pledge or vow to be publicly acknowledged before witnesses and before God.

Oaths, pledges and vows share the same purpose. They all demand the courage of our convictions. They all need to be taken seriously, otherwise we should do away with them. Why have them if we are not serious about abiding by and enforcing them? This is a matter of principle.

Apparently, though, the issue for many boils down to semantic hairsplitting. Many consider a violation of an oath of office much more serious than a violation of a marriage vow, apparently because they see the former as a legal dilemma, the latter as only a moral dilemma. After all, failure to abide by your oath of office could lead to serious legal ramifications including prison for dereliction of duty, treason, bribery or other criminal acts of negligence or malfeasance. On the other hand, a failed marriage is not criminal behavior, and can only lead to separation or divorce. People who share this view see no moral connection to their vow of marriage before God.

Regardless of whether it is a legal or a moral dilemma, Americans should expect a full commitment to the ideals of the oath, pledge or vow. How else can we have a fully functioning, civil society?

What of other commitments, like giving your word? Is a promise, without a special, publicly acknowledged commitment, still a solemn pledge? Of course it is, but many see a broken promise in the same manner they see a broken contract. "If circumstances change, then I'm allowed to renege on my previous promise."

We have become a nation that regards all obligations in terms of legality, not in terms of morality. We don't connect the dots between oaths of office, vows of marriage, or pledges of support as a solemn agreement of our word before God as our witness. This lack of connection needs to change if we expect oaths, vows and pledges to have significant meaning in the future.

Chapter 8: The Purpose of Character

Character is defined as moral integrity, a strict adherence to a standard of value or conduct pertaining to the principles of right and wrong.

Character counts!

How often have we heard those two words?

Our character reflects the values we aspire to uphold. Character is our very being. It describes who we are, what we are all about. Character defines our reputation. We are known for the character traits that we possess, by the values that we truly cherish.

For example, Mother Teresa is known worldwide for her compassion, love and understanding, and she has been characterized as saintly for her unselfish devotion to the downtrodden among us. Adolph Hitler, on the other hand, is known for his ruthlessness and the racist views of his definition of the so-called Aryan race. He has been accurately characterized as a brutal, cruel and evil tyrant. Embracing entirely different moral standards, Mother Teresa and Adolph Hitler were both known for the charismatic character they projected to the masses.

So does character count? How could it not! Mother Teresa has gone down in history as a saint, Hitler as little more than a demented, mass murderer.

Many Americans, particularly younger Americans, don't yet understand that their character is viewed as a reflection of the kind of people they are. Their character is judged—rightfully or wrongfully—by what they value, by what they wear and even by what they endorse. They don't understand why some adults view their impudent behavior with skepticism. They sense they are being targeted (or profiled) because of their actions or conduct or what they wear—for no reason at all. Most likely, of course, they are targeted for the character they are projecting, their image as we see them, not as they see themselves.

For better or for worse, this is how I judge people, and I suspect most Americans do the same.

If young people wear T-shirts endorsing Ice T or other recording artists whose lyrics support killing cops and raping women, I see this as a reflection of their values (or perhaps the values of their parents). If they wear gang colors or clothing emblazoned with images of illegal drugs or with raunchy phrases, it leaves the impression that they are thugs and people to watch carefully. I believe most Americans feel this same way, but many will deny it because they don't want to be seen as judgmental.

But perception does count. If I perceive you to be a threat because of what you are wearing or how you are acting, I will certainly be more cautious around you. And there is nothing wrong with a healthy skepticism; it may just save my life or avert injury. Even Jesse Jackson once remarked that he was relieved after hearing footsteps behind him when he turned around to see white faces. Apparently, because of the part of town he was walking in, he perceived he was in danger. But why was he relieved when he saw "white faces?" Perhaps he "perceived" that white faces wouldn't harm him in this area of town. Why else would he have been "judgmental," and how did he know that these "white faces" wouldn't do him harm? Was he "profiling" young black thugs?

The politically correct crowd—members of the liberal left who claim to be non-judgmental—often are quite judgmental on the basis of perception of character. Why else do they claim that those of us against quotas for affirmative action are insensitive or even racist, simply because we value merit over quotas? They apparently perceive that the character traits that we value—hard work and meeting minimum standards—are threats to their agenda. So in effect, haven't they "profiled" us by what we say, what we do and to what organizations we belong?

Similarly, when the police force "profiles" character traits that represent criminal behavior, aren't they often labeled racists? And when a store clerk "profiles" a group of teenagers in his store because of their conduct or gang dress, isn't he classified as insensitive?

But let's face it, we all classify people because of their dress, conduct and affiliation. Years ago we might imagine the man with a pager was a doctor, today we might think he is a drug dealer. Nuns are classified as holy by their dress, Osama Bin Laden as a terrorist by his conduct, and Ku Klux Klan members as racists because of their affiliation. But the bottom line is that our character classifies us whether we like it or not, and people "judge" us because of how we look, what we wear, how we eat,

what we say, what we believe in and the organizations to
which we belong.

But some view this natural process of "judging"
people's character as flawed because it requires us to
compare right and wrong behavior based upon a common
standard of decency. The problem, then, lies in our
personal standards of right and wrong. What I consider
wrong behavior may not meet your definition. Your curse
words may infuriate me but simply be slang words to you.
My children may not understand why your children "get
away" with conduct I deplore in them. What I consider
incivility may clearly be no big deal to you. I may view
your behavior as boorish; you may view it as simply an
expression of who you are.
    Nevertheless, we are all entitled to expect a certain
level of common decency directed towards one another.
That common decency, known as a code of conduct, has
historical roots in religious faiths and early governments.

The early Roman Empire established its own code of
conduct. In the Judeo-Christian faith, that code of conduct
is known as the Ten Commandments. There is even a
book, written when my children were little, entitled *All I
Ever Needed to Know I Learned in Kindergarten,* that
describes in childlike fashion the tenets of decent behavior.
    Therefore, with all this guidance, why can't we be civil
to one another? Why can't we embody the virtues in the
Ten Commandments? Can we even list the Ten
Commandments? My guess is that we have forgotten or
never really learned of their existence.
    The point is that we do have faith-based standards of
decency and other established rules of behavior to follow;
but for many of us, we have simply elected to ignore them.
And as I delineated earlier in this chapter, your character
reflects the values you choose to live by, and you either

live by those values or you do not. You can not elect to endorse some of them, neglecting others and then claim you have an intact value system of right and wrong. Sounds similar to "situational ethics," doesn't it?

Ted Turner (of CNN, TBS and TNT television fame and husband of Jane Fonda) recently engaged in "situational ethics" in regard to the Ten Commandments. He declared that if you are only going to have Ten Commandments, adultery should probably not be one of them. He later apologized, but he obviously doesn't consider this Judeo-Christian code of conduct in general, and adultery in particular, to be an important dimension of his character. I assume he thought his casual disregard for the Ten Commandments to be his private, personal belief. And that's all right, but it certainly reflects upon his character in my view.

Similarly, President Clinton's defenders claim the same thing. They claim that what went on in the Oval Office between the President and Monica Lewinsky was private, not public, business. I could argue that the White House, other than the private living quarters, is a public office building paid for by the taxpayers.

But that's not my point.

We're talking about character. Regardless of whether you think Ted Turner's comments or President Clinton's actions in the Oval Office are public or private affairs, it's their character in both scenarios that remains the same. We can not claim that there is no character flaw simply because we have decided that the action was private and not public. Remember, character refers to moral integrity, not public or private conduct. We cannot possess a public character that is different from our private character. They are one and the same: a set of values, which defines our reputation. Character can not be separated or compartmentalized. Therefore, you must conclude as I have, that character does count!

But is it really that important a quality to possess?

Of course it is. Would you hire somebody with serious character flaws?_

Let's assume you are about to hire an employee to direct one of your special projects, which includes managing a large budget. Wouldn't you like to know that the employee you are about to hire has the utmost integrity, honesty, and trustworthiness? Don't you think that the private and public aspects of his life should be well known to you? Would it bother you to find out later that he has a drug problem, but claims he only abuses drugs on his own time? Would it concern you if the lady you are about to hire as the comptroller had serious money problems and had declared bankruptcy?

The answers to these questions go to the very heart of the character issue, and they can have a serious affect upon your company's reputation.

The Democratic spin machine has trivialized the character issue to the point that many of us have become convinced that character flaws are unimportant in a leader. The polls tell us that the general public is not concerned with the President's character as long as the economy is good to them. Why worry about something you have no control over anyway? Besides, why care what the President does in his private life (assuming you agree that his conduct in the Oval Office was a private affair)?

How can people think this?

The general public rightly buys into the notion that private conduct should remain private. In fact, private individuals feel they should be more insulated than public officials concerning scrutiny of their behavior. And I concur, as long as that conduct remains in the private domain. However, once that conduct is in the public domain because it is illegal or has adversely affected the lives of other people, then public scrutiny is warranted.

Yet, lots of people don't understand that distinction. That's why many of them gave President Clinton a pass for his reprehensible behavior. They continue to believe it was a private, consensual affair. It has not occurred to them that perhaps it was actually illegal behavior. And indeed, many lawyers still think that the President could be charged with violating the rule of law in the District of Columbia after he leaves office.

And if character counts as I suggest it does, then why do we continue to tolerate "situational ethics" when we allow celebrity athletes with serious character flaws to continue to play the game. It just doesn't make any sense to me. Let me give you a few examples.

Peter Warrick is a wide receiver for the Florida State Seminoles and was a leading contender for the Heisman Trophy. He recently was caught, along with a teammate, buying designer clothes at a mall department store for a fraction of the cost from another FSU classmate who was the store clerk. According to Peter Warrick, he had done this once or twice before. Although charged with a felony, the case was reduced to a misdemeanor and he was reinstated to the football team after missing two games. His teammate was not so lucky. He was permanently suspended from the team because of prior team infractions and run-ins with law enforcement officers.

To many Seminoles' football fans, Peter Warrick was being convicted over a trivial matter. They simply claimed that he ought to be able to pay the full price of the clothing he received and get on with his life. It didn't matter to them that he was caught on camera committing a felony (as opposed to a misdemeanor) crime.

When an initial plea bargain (delayed 30 day jail sentence after the season) reached the president of the university, he rightly stated that Peter Warrick could not play football while awaiting the sentence for a felony conviction to begin. Suddenly, that felony, which had been caught on tape, was reduced to a misdemeanor and Peter Warrick was allowed to resume his college football career. I have to wonder how many big time boosters got involved in the sudden decision to reduce the charge.

My point in this illustration is simple. One athlete, who was easily replaced on the team by another player, was kicked off the team for committing the same felony that the other more prominent, Heisman Trophy candidate also committed. The Athletic Department did not see the character issue as being central. They rationalized their decision to their advantage claiming one athlete had previous offenses, the other did not. But apparently not all of the university authorities believed they ought to hold both athletes responsible for their actions. One player was kicked off the team, while Peter Warrick—the more famous and valuable of the two—was allowed to remain. Someone in a position of power displayed a lack of character, using situational ethics to justify a questionable decision.

Mike Tyson is a famous boxer. He is an equally famous prison inmate. He was convicted of raping a young beauty pageant contestant and was sent to prison. Upon release from prison, Mike Tyson went back to work in the boxing ring. Once again he found himself in trouble because he bit part of Evander Holyfield's ear off during a fight. We're not talking about a low blow or a sucker punch; we're talking about biting off an ear, an assault on another boxer in the ring before the cameras. For this infraction, the boxing commission withdrew his license to fight.

Still later, during a minor traffic mishap on the

Maryland highways, Iron Mike lost it again by assaulting two older men after they had rear-ended the car his wife was driving at the time. Instead of handling this minor traffic mishap in a mature manner, the volatile Mike Tyson assaulted the two men. For violating his parole, he was sent back to a Maryland jail for additional time.

So the question now is, should Mike Tyson be allowed to fight again? Should the boxing commission reinstate his license for a second time? How many chances does he get? His defenders say he has a right to work. I agree. But does that mean he has to get back into the ring?

What was the Nevada State Boxing Commission thinking about when they returned him to the ring? What was their purpose for doing so? Why did they remove his license in the first place? If the act was so egregious to cause them to remove his license, what has he done since then to justify them reinstating it? Mike Tyson has only proven to me that he is mentally immature and unstable in and out of the ring.

There is a similar case of assault involving Latrell Sprewell, then of the Golden State Warriors of the NBA. The team suspended him for one year—later reduced to the remainder of the season by the league—for assaulting his coach during a basketball practice session. He apparently had left the court after arguing with P. J. Carlesimo, the head coach of the Warriors, only to return to choke him. Was this not premeditated assault on his coach?

Latrell Sprewell is a fantastic basketball player, but he obviously has some character flaws, including a violent temper. Since there was no chance that he would return to play for the coach, he was later traded to the New York Knicks and signed a huge salary contract. But does he deserve a second chance like that given to Mike Tyson? Perhaps, but at the salary he got from the Knicks? What was the Knicks' management thinking about when they hired Latrell Sprewell at that salary? It surely wasn't about the team reputation. It must have been all about winning and not about reputation (or character).

In this case I believe Latrell Sprewell deserves a second chance. He has apologized and he appears to be contrite. My only problem is rewarding him with a huge contract. It doesn't say much for the Knicks' management decision.

And what about the fans? Is the character issue important to them, or is winning the championship all they really care about?

Unlike the rest of the Knicks basketball team, Latrell Sprewell did not attend training camp this year, apparently for his own personal reasons. Naturally he was available for the start of the season, and he received a standing ovation from the New York crowd. What does this say about New York sports fans in general? And, of course, it also re-enforces bad behavior on the part of Latrell Sprewell, whose ego swells even more.

Another case illustrating my point involves Lawrence Taylor, the former All-Pro linebacker with the New York Giants football team. Lawrence Taylor was selected in his first year of eligibility to the National Football League Hall of Fame. But does he deserve to be enshrined? Yes, he had Hall of Fame numbers, but did you know he was a convicted felon for drug abuse. In fact, since retirement from football, he has had several run-ins with law enforcement officials for drug problems. Of course his defenders say his performance on the field should be the criterion, not what he does in his private life. (Are illegal drug abuse and a prison sentence considered part of private life?)

Unlike major league baseball, the NFL Hall of Fame guidelines have no clause about personal responsibility off the field. It's what he did on the field that counts. So sorry, Pete Rose. In my view, at least, baseball has some decency to establish a standard of right and wrong behavior, on and off the field.

What were the voters (Board of Selectors) for the NFL Hall of Fame thinking about when they selected Lawrence Taylor? The rules don't prohibit him from earning a place in the Hall of Fame for his off field antics, therefore, it was perfectly legal to install him with the other great football players who played by the rules.

But I don't accept that proposition. Just because it is legal doesn't make it right.

Thank goodness some of those writers had the integrity to say his off field behavior should not be condoned, and they did not vote for his selection.

Where does it stop? What if, instead of abusing drugs, Lawrence Taylor committed armed robbery or murder? Would that have changed the vote? Should he still be enshrined? Or are drug offenses the only acceptable felony to be admitted into the professional football Hall of Fame?

What about O. J. Simpson? He was enshrined in the football Hall of Fame, and later was convicted in a civil trial for murdering his ex-wife. Should he now be removed? Or should his biography on display be updated to reflect his true character? Does the football Hall of Fame committee desire this type of image to be portrayed to the millions of youngsters who visit the Hall each year? Is O. J's character on display, or is it the committee's character on display?

Unfortunately, the pro football Hall of Fame only includes the on field statistics and a few personal items of its 199 members. That's a shame. Why not include their full character? Why not display their off-field activities and life after football?

Another pro football Hall of Famer, Alan Page, has a

stellar biography, on and off the field. He is currently a Minnesota Supreme Court Justice. Doesn't it seem important to tout his off field endeavors, particularly his truly successful achievement as a Justice of the Supreme Court of Minnesota? Perhaps the National Football League would care to address these issues. Perhaps they would like to provide us with the purpose for not changing the guidelines to include off field behavior in voting for new members.

Or is this just another "situational ethics" thing?

But back to Pete Rose. Since Major League Baseball has an off field clause on character, should they make an exception for "Charlie Hustle?" Why should he be singled out among the one hundred great athletes of the century as one who has not been elected to his sports' Hall of Fame? Perhaps character does matter once in awhile.

But you sure couldn't tell that to NBC sports reporter Jim Gray. Jim Gray interviewed Pete Rose during the 1999 World Series when all the living athletes who were able to attend the ceremony were honored. Unfortunately for Jim Gray, the fans, the media and the Yankee ball players all ostracized him for his insistent and demanding questioning of Pete Rose's ethical standing caused by his gambling on major league baseball games. Although Pete Rose continues to deny he gambled on the Cincinnati Reds, a team he managed at the time, Jim Gray, in my opinion was after a story. Nothing negative would have been said about Jim Gray if he got the "scoop" and Pete Rose finally admitted to his mistake. However, since Pete Rose continued to deny he bet on baseball, the media and the fans declared Jim Gray to be overly aggressive in attempting to find out the "truth" about a legitimate story.

To complicate matters more, the media insisted that Jim Gray was actually ruining a very special day for the all-time hits leader, and that his actions were way out of line. Even the members of the Yankee clubhouse later refused to conduct interviews with Jim Gray, the NBC reporter assigned to conduct them.

You may argue that Jim Gray went too far during the interview, especially knowing full well that Pete Rose failed to answer the question. But let's all agree that everyone who refused to talk with Jim Gray, and the fans and the media alike who adamantly denounced him for doing so, were not interested in the character issue at all. To them, Pete Rose is a hero, and the big, bad Major League Baseball Association is a heartless organization that should change its archaic rules.

I hope it doesn't.

Jim Gray was trying to do his job, and as far as I am concerned, he showed more character than all the others involved in this sorry escapade.

I'll bet we can do better. We can change the way the pro football Hall of Fame selection is conducted if we really wanted to change it. It's up to us to persuade the members of the Hall of Fame selection committee to change their guidelines for enshrinement. They need to reevaluate their purpose for selection.

I know I previously said private organizations have the right to decide upon their own rules and regulations, but that doesn't mean we shouldn't try to persuade them to think about character.

Should it really be about inducting those athletes who have the God-given ability to run, pass, kick and catch; or should it reflect a Hall of Heroes whom we all can look up to with pride and inspiration in their athletic ability and their strength of character?

Congressman J. C. Watts of Oklahoma once remarked that character is doing the right thing when nobody is looking. He's right, of course.

How many times have we seen politicians deny

allegations which surface through press reports, only to acknowledge them when evidence is presented (as did Bill Clinton when his DNA was revealed on a certain dress that did not belong to his wife). Even then words are parsed to lessen the offense.

If we tell the truth the first time and every time, we need never have to lie. Unfortunately, those people with character flaws try endlessly never to have to admit they are wrong. They rationalize their own actions by playing the "blame game."

Thomas Babington Macaulay, a famous English historian, poet and essayist from the mid-1800s, said it best: "The measure of a man's real character is what he would do if he knew he never would be found out."

*"What gives life its value
you can find—and lose. But
never possess. This holds
good above all for the Truth
about Life."*
Dag Hammarskjöld

Chapter 9: The
Purpose of Values

*The purpose of values is to establish a core of
desirable, worthwhile and recognizable standards of
behavior known as common decency.*

Normally when we refer to values we tend to think
of material worth, such as the price or cost of goods and
services; or we tend to think of something or someone's
usefulness to us.

For example, I might place an extraordinary value
(material worth) on my antique sports car if I were a car
buff; or I would value (find useful) your support for my
business proposal if I were getting ready to go into business
for myself.

Many Americans tend to value anything or anybody

that will provide benefit to them politically, socially, or commercially. They are driven more today by material worth, greed and "wanting to have it all" that is measured in dollars, votes or power, than by acts of common decency or moral convictions that show little in the way of value as defined by material worth or usefulness.

But there is another far more important, yet more obscure meaning of the term "values," a meaning that has become blurred with the lack of emphasis today on moral convictions. Other than the sense of doing the right thing for the right reasons and feeling good inside, common decency yields no instant wealth or power or value in the traditional sense of the word.

For example, I find myself frustrated with people on the street or in the hallways who ignore my "Good Morning." In my opinion, a response is just plain common courtesy. To me, it simply reflects their lack of politeness.

Should I really care? Perhaps I'm being overly concerned, but I also sense that this behavior (assuming they just didn't hear me) reflects an uncivil attitude towards a fellow human being, or at least an uncaring attitude.

Yes, I *am* being judgmental again.

There are many other examples of common decency that have been placed on the endangered list during my lifetime.

I was taught well by my parents to respect my elders, to say "Ma'am" and "Sir," to open doors for ladies, to wait for all to be served at a restaurant before eating, and to offer my seat on a bus to the elderly or to a woman. This is basic common courtesy and politeness (feminists might say chauvinistic).

These were values ingrained in me as a child to re-enforce good behavior as an adult. Small sacrifices learned early on in life helped re-enforce friendship and cooperation later on in life.

Today this behavior is considered silly or not "cool." In reality, what has happened over time is that the coarseness of our culture has eroded our politeness and common courtesy and values. We no longer see these acts as politeness, or decency, or being considerate of others; we see them as "valueless."

What do I gain in giving my seat to an elderly gentleman on the bus? That means I must stand the next thirty minutes to my destination, and besides, I got here first. If I wait until everyone is served a meal, my food will get cold, and besides, I'm hungry.

These acts of common courtesy I just described, although minor in nature, have nearly disappeared and have been replaced with far more serious breaches of misbehavior.

Pop culture with its themes of "me first"—raw entertainment that considers rudeness as "cool"—and the lack of morality manifested in nudity, swearing and violence on our big and small screens, has nearly obliterated the values associated with common decency.

Consider road rage.

For heaven's sake, if I were not going to open the door for that lady with the baby stroller, why on earth would I let her into the flow of traffic, especially if it makes me miss the next light. And if she tries to cut in because nobody has the courtesy to let her in, then I'm entitled to "road rage."

Sure I get annoyed at the driver who drives slowly in the fast lane, but what good does it do me to "flip him off" or squeal around him only to slam on my brakes in front of him to teach him a lesson?

My point is that formerly common acts of decency, requiring nothing more than to be courteous to one another, have fallen by the wayside because they are no longer taught or "valued" in a society that ignores their meaning. If we can't even hold open a door for an unknown stranger, why would we be courteous to our next door neighbor whom we have probably known longer? If we don't respect our grandparents' life-styles and values because they are old fogies and out of touch, then why would we help a coworker who possesses different cultural values than our own?

My point, again, is that if we are not taught these basic standards of common decency, and to respect others viewpoints and life-styles, we will simply add to the incivility in the nation.

Treat others, as you would like to be treated. Remember that phrase? If all we ever did were to treat others, as we would like to be treated, common courtesy would return.

The problem with most people, including me, is that we forget that phrase. We get so annoyed with misbehavior and lack of politeness that we either imitate it to get even, or we totally ignore it and let it fester. Rather, what we need to do is to politely confront it where we can and get control of the situation.

At the risk of being called "holier than thou," and with just a few moments of observation, I can identify which families encourage values-based morality and common decency, simply by their children's behavior in public. Their encouragement is evident in the politeness (versus rudeness) and courtesy (versus inconsiderateness) demonstrated by their children's respect for others.

Some will argue that politeness and common courtesy mean little; no one is harmed by bad manners, rude jokes and comments which just poke a little fun at someone's expense; and besides, it's only their feelings that are hurt, they'll "get over it."

But consider this: a lack of respect for others, be it

based on their life-style, age, religion, ethnicity, or physical features, clearly encourages an equal lack of respect for company policy, safety issues, coworkers' appearance, fraud, waste, and reputation. We cannot separate our values towards others from the values we show towards our own company or neighborhood.

Values are values; either we possess them in varying degrees, or we do not. We can change them, we can improve on them, we can ignore them, but we cannot possess a set for our public life that is different from those in our personal life.

Just as with character, values reflect our reputation. That's why in the past society imposed recognizable standards of behavior for all to aspire to.

It has only been in the last twenty to thirty years that we have disregarded our older values and let our current valueless culture erode our standards of behavior.

To illustrate my point further, let's look at the advertising industry and prime time television programming, which includes adult cartoons and so called "family sitcoms." Remember the early days of television when nudity was a rarity, profanity was seldom heard, and sexual innuendo was nonexistent?

Those days are certainly gone, apparently forever.

In today's "valueless" society, cable and network executives think they have absolved themselves from responsibility by simply adding a disclaimer up front during the credits. But what have they really done by being so "responsible"?

They have acknowledged that not everyone should see their programming, but rather than blaming themselves for producing it, they lay the blame on those who watch it! Pretty clever ploy!

In reality, of course, they know full well what a hormone-raging teenager will focus on. What these executives fail to recognize or totally disregard is the purpose of their programming. What they will not admit is that they lack morals themselves, they don't want to be judgmental, and they are strictly focused on profits and television ratings shares.

Years ago we had advertising such as "Bucky Beaver" for Ipana toothpaste with his "...brusha... brusha...brusha..." song.

Innocent, fun, and it got the point across. Today we have sensual underwear ads and Nike's "Just Do It" ads. It's brazen and "in your face" talk that sells, but it clearly is valueless, promotes a pornographic view of women, and lacks focus on respect.

Ever notice the staccato-like, tough, in-your-face voice used in radio and television advertising, selling everything from beer to cars? Radio and television advertising executives have jumped all over this type of advertising, apparently because it sells with the younger crowd who think there is nothing wrong in "dissing" one another. Many must think this is "cool." I think this is disrespectful.

In my youth we had great television family hours which had a recognizable theme: good behavior and teaching morals. The children who starred in "Father Knows Best" and "Ozzie and Harriet" often were in trouble because they were still learning to become successful adults, but their parents (with the executives and screenwriters) emphasized right and common decency over wrong.

Can we say the same thing about "Married with Children" and "The Simpsons"? Father figures were prominent in my youth, usually as heroes.

Look at the way the bumbling, idiotic fathers are presented today. Look at the way authority figures in general are portrayed in television and movies today. They are either crooked, or buffoons or they lack morals themselves.

Screenwriters, rather than focusing on the majority of kindhearted, righteous authority figures serving our nation, focus on a few wayward priests, crooked cops, or "on the take" politicians. But—surprise, surprise—the majority of these professionals are not at all as they appear on the screen. However, this is what sells! Why? Because, we are a "valueless" society.

If this type of programming and advertising doesn't bother you, if it doesn't get under your skin a little bit, then I suggest that your "values" may be getting a little fuzzy.

If we think that society in general is better off because of this type of advertising and entertainment programming, then I suggest that perhaps we need to reassess our values as they relate to common decency. And if we do not want to admit that the brazen, in-your-face, constant drumbeat of nudity, profanity and violence in the entertainment industry programming does not affect our society's behavior and attitude towards one another, then tell me why we have popular, long-running children's programming such as "Sesame Street"? What would be its purpose?

If we claim, as entertainment executives admit, that good children's programming can be a good stimulus for children, why don't they admit that other programming may be bad for them? I don't get it! How can they have it both ways? This clearly is another attempt at "situational ethics".

If, as I suggest, we cannot separate our public "character" from our private "character," or our public "values" from our private "values", then how can we separate the thought that good children's programming can positively influence children's behavior, but other programming does not?

Respect for values comes from one's heart, mind and soul. They can not be separated.

> "The legitimate object of government is to do for a community of people whatever they need to have done, but cannot do at all in their separate and individual capacities."
> **Abraham Lincoln**

Chapter 10: The Purpose of Government

The purpose of government is to provide for the common defense and the welfare and safety of its citizenry.

What is the purpose of government? Have we, as a nation governed by the people and for the people, really taken the time to think about the purpose of government? Or are we so self-absorbed in our own little worlds that we automatically accept the mandates that government imposes upon us in countless seen and unseen ways? Have we really tried to understand the impact of various executive orders, legislative policies, or judicial decisions? Are we truly informed?

My guess is that most Americans are so busy earning a living and squiring children around town they do not have a real clue as to what governmental programs are paid for with their tax dollars. They do not understand how much governmental power at all levels is vested in special interests, lobbyists and career bureaucrats and staffers.

A fundamental truth about government and politics is that policies are pursued on the basis of interest alone. Think about it. No policy would ever be enacted if there were no interest in it. But lobbyists and activists, who may or may not represent the majority of Americans, are paid by their organizations to stir up interest (and donations to campaign war chests) in order to obtain a favorable advantage for their clients. Most Americans could care less, until after the fact, when it comes time to pay the bills in the form of raised taxes, increased spending or deficit reduction that hurts our pet programs.

What we fail to understand is the complete scope of government. Have we ever really sat down and thought about what the government's scope of responsibility ought to be? Have we ever made a list of responsibilities or priorities that the federal, state or local government ought to do for its citizens? Have we ever thought that perhaps some of the responsibilities that government has usurped are either outdated, inefficient, or fail to represent the broader society and instead represent special interest groups solely? Has the government gone overboard in setting up special commissions, task forces and bureaucracies in an attempt to satisfy every constituent and special interest group in our community?

I'm not suggesting that all government programs or bureaucracies be eliminated, but I am suggesting that some of them serve no purpose for the good of society as a whole. They were primarily established to support special interest groups in a sincere effort to be "fair" to all citizens. But at what cost? Now is the time to reevaluate the purpose behind every existing program and policy, and to look to the future with a new approach of analyzing before enacting.

The federal government has grown so large that it is nearly impossible to operate effectively all its cabinet level departments, branches, agencies and commissions. According to the Senior Executives Association, there have been sixteen new titled layers of government (deputy to the Deputy Secretary; principal assistant deputy to the Under Secretary; associate principal deputy; etc.) created in the last six years of the Clinton administration?

The sad reality is that we do not even know where our federal tax dollars are going and for what purpose. Look at the recent fiasco at the Internal Revenue Service. The same bureaucracy that requires us to know thousands of pages of tax code rules and regulations and then accurately report them on our tax returns in a timely fashion, is the same organization that miserably failed its own audit conducted by the General Accounting Office. The GAO, a congressional oversight organization, reported that the IRS inefficiently performed its function as the nation's tax collector, by failing to keep track of the billions of dollars owed to the federal government by the taxpayers. Even worse, they failed to keep track of the money appropriated to them by Congress for overhead, operating expenses, salary and the like. In other words, they failed miserably as a business. Even more perplexing to me than the results of the audit, was the length of time that this inefficiency was allowed to continue. Where was the Congressional oversight years ago?

To my mind, the oversight was an amazing discovery. Just think how much money was wasted. And nobody cared enough to stop the waste until there was an audit ordered by Congress! Think anybody will lose his job over his failure to be accountable? The IRS is only one of many federal agencies which receive appropriated funds from the Congress to do the nation's business. These agencies need to be held accountable for their business practices, just as we are held accountable for ours.

Consider the likely inefficiencies, fraud and other wasteful practices that exist in other federal organizations. The Department of Defense has probably been audited more times than any other cabinet level department in the federal government. A few years back the Defense Department revised its acquisition development programs to curtail such practices as spending six hundred dollars on an aircraft toilet seat that had to meet military specifications or that required buying expensive replacement parts under contract that could be purchased significantly cheaper at a local hardware store.

But acquisition reform is easy compared to changing the infrastructure.

The service chiefs, who would prefer to raise their member's salaries and modernize their weapons systems, have repeatedly asked for another round of base closings to reduce their overhead. But the political machine and the local officials in each district where jobs may be lost due to base closure, lobby against that argument. Their argument is for political purposes, not necessarily for business purposes.

Recently the House of Representatives Government Reform and Oversight Subcommittee on Government Management, Information and Technology issued its second annual report on the status of the 24 cabinet level departments and 70 related agencies and how they conduct the nation's business. Although showing improvement from the previous year, only 24 agencies met the accounting standards acceptable to the General Accounting Office of the Congress. That means 46 federal agencies are not in compliance. And worse, it is reported that $1.8 trillion dollars of our taxpayer money spent on various programs cannot be accounted for, and an additional $1.6 trillion dollars in capital equipment, parts and supplies is unaccounted for, totaling $3.4 trillion (not billion) dollars in fraud, waste or mismanagement by the federal government alone. That's disgraceful. Just imagine what we could do with $3.4 trillion dollars. In addition, the *Washington Times* reports that for the first time in more than 200 years, Congress must now accurately report the net cost of running the government. I haven't seen the results yet, but I doubt we'll be impressed by the government's efficiency.

Corporations restructure all the time. They close inefficient plants as necessary. Why can't the government reduce its inventory of land, facilities and personnel? Are you familiar with any cabinet level department other than Defense, which in the last few years has conducted a sweeping audit of its land, facilities and personnel infrastructure?

Why is it we feel free to add new programs, with associated infrastructure and budgets, but we never feel free to disband them? It is time to hold our government accountable. We should demand that all levels of government eliminate fraud, waste and abuse and inefficient infrastructure.

On a grand scale, do we really need 24 Cabinet level departments and 70 agencies, plus all the bureaus, task forces and commissions? I'm not convinced that we do. Have the taxpayers benefited from the Department of Housing and Urban Development which recently had its emergency funds frozen by Congress to prevent the department from just spending those funds? Isn't housing a local matter? Do we really need an Energy Department? Do we have any idea of the annual budget appropriated for each of the above bureaucracies? Do we know how many people they employ? Do we know the number of buildings they occupy? Do we know how many dollars in their budget go to support infrastructure, salary or programs? Do we know how many other similar programs exist in other federal agencies?

For example, did you know that there are 35 federal laws governing food safety in 12 different federal agencies? The Department of Agriculture is responsible for inspecting food plants that produce open-faced meat sandwiches and pizza with a meat topping, but the Department of Health and Human Services Food and Drug Administration inspects food plants that produce regular meat sandwiches and non-meat pizzas. That's absurd! It is estimated that $30 billion a year is wasted on everything from food stamp fraud (a one billion dollar a year program) to inefficient food safety inspections. And each agency is vying for its fair share of the federal budget! Why not combine some or all of these functions and perhaps have one pizza czar inspector? Or should we continue to duplicate these functions purely to satisfy the existing bureaucrats holding down these jobs so we don't put them out of work?

It's not enough just to declare war by "reinventing government" as Vice President Al Gore has done. This effort should be much more than just reducing the number of instructions and publications and government regulations. It's time to clean house. Get rid of those functions that can easily be absorbed into other departments or done more efficiently at the state level. Analyze the cost to benefit ratio of a program to determine if it is truly a worthwhile benefit for society as a whole or if it exists just to satisfy the special interests of lobbyists and activists. We must demand that our governmental supervisors and managers, who are responsible and accountable for the programs under their purview, reevaluate the purpose of their program's existence.

When was the last time anyone from government completed a cost-benefit ratio for each program they manage? When was the last time anyone from government actually canceled a program while working on it?

Let me give you a quick story about a program that I was managing for the Navy headquarters staff in the Pentagon during the early '80s. I managed the disposition of excess Navy and Marine Corps aircraft that were stored at the Military Aircraft Storage and Disposition Center in Tucson, Arizona. This site was used because the dry desert climate was conducive to maintaining the integrity of aircraft systems. Twice yearly, military and civilian personnel would assemble for three days in Tucson for the purpose of determining the status of aircraft disposition, whether to continue to store aircraft, strike them from the rolls, or return them to active duty.

After my first visit, I determined that this was an unnecessary waste of valuable time and money to hold a twice yearly, three-day conference to accomplish what I considered could be done in several hours over a few days by telephone. However, I could not get the bureaucracy to change a system that had been in place for years. When the Navy headquarters staff finally decided to enact my recommendation to save dollars and reduce the conference to an annual event over two days, the bureaucrats (particularly the entrenched civilians) at the Naval Air Systems Command convinced their senior leadership to continue funding a twice-yearly conference.

Are you surprised?

Business managers constantly review policies and programs to become more efficient and ensure they make a profit for their stockholders, but bureaucrats, on the other hand, only manage a budget given to them. Business managers look for profits; bureaucrats look for dollars—your dollars.

There is an interesting phenomenon about layered government. If the Feds put in a new program, then the states are likely to have a similar arrangement in order to have an office capable of complying with all the red tape that surely will follow; likewise with the county seats and city councils. It's like a contagious disease!

For example, for every new cabinet level agency that has been established in my lifetime, there has been a corresponding increase in the number of state and city level offices to support them.

When President Jimmy Carter proposed the Department of Education as a new cabinet-level agency in the '70s, the states soon followed suit. Similarly, the state of Florida established a Veterans' Affairs office as a cabinet level political appointee of the governor to support federal mandates from the U.S. Department of Veterans' Affairs office in Washington, D.C. Many states have the same, right down to the level of county Veterans' Affairs Officers!

Do we really need all these positions? Are they really necessary?

The veterans will claim a resounding yes, but veterans compose a very small proportion of the American population. Are we pandering to a special constituency? And if that sounds callous (I am a veteran of two wars), were we insensitive to the veterans of WWI and WWII years ago when we didn't have a special cabinet level office for their needs? Of course not! The difference today lies in all the associations that are willing to lobby the U.S. government for special benefits for our warriors. I see nothing wrong with supporting the troops who faithfully supported our government's foreign policy. My point is that if we decide veterans need a spokesman in the government, why can't we establish an office in the Department of Defense rather than an entire bureaucracy?

The state of Florida has 23 executive branch departments, almost matching the federal government in scope. Additionally, it supports innumerable commissions and agencies to conduct the people's business. State and local governments have become just as bloated as the federal government, but at least they tend to be much more efficient because voters scrutinize their budgets much more closely.

That's the good news.

But when state or local governments are strapped for money, they simply apply for federal funds because they know there is a readily available "cash cow", because the state's Congressional delegations are more than eager to support these requests.

The problem with states accepting federal bailouts is twofold. First, it inevitably leads to federal mandates and guidelines on just how the expenditure of those funds must be applied. Second, and perhaps more pernicious, is the fact that federal funds become almost a requirement to sustain previous spending levels.

No politician wants to turn down federal money because it eases the burden on state spending.

But the reality is that no matter who pays for the program, state or federal, neither government reached into its piggy bank to pay for it. Rather, it came out of your pocket. State or federal government either had to increase taxes on the populace, reduce spending on other programs, or borrow money and add to the debt to pay for the principal and interest, getting even further into your pocket.

The fact remains, and it is still my contention, that

the majority of people in any given community don't have a clue as to where their local and state tax dollars are spent and for what purpose. They are not aware of the existence of many tax-draining programs, nor do they know the extent these programs will cost them through additional taxation, increased spending or borrowing. Ask yourself these questions. What was the purpose of the last bond floated by your city council? Was it to raise the dollars necessary to help defray the costs of an entrepreneur to bring in a professional sports team? If so, is that the purpose of city government? Why should you pay the cost of someone else's private enterprise?

It may be a very wise decision to bring in a professional sports team to enhance the city's image, boost morale and bring in needed dollars for the city's coffers and other business opportunities. But let's not forget that the city's charter (or constitution) must ensure that we meet the basic requirements for its citizenry before we meet the demands of a few organizers, sympathizers and advocates for professional sports. In short, we must understand the purpose of the bond and determine if that money would be better spent on highway or bridge construction, improving school infrastructure or developing mass transit.

It's not just legislators and well-connected lobbyists who force the taxpayers to foot the bill. Judicial decisions, based upon ideological agendas, often mandate citizens to spend federal, state or local dollars to improve infrastructure that perhaps the citizenry has previously rejected. Some judges, without regard to cost, require municipalities, cities or states to comply with their mandates. Take for example Judge Russell Clark's decision to impose upon the citizens of the Kansas City, Missouri School District, his interpretation of what the public schools should do for capital improvements. According to the Court Jester Awards, Judge Clark determined that racially segregated schools should be improved to attract white students. He got personally involved and required his approval before replacing carpeting or even painting the school walls. Is that the purpose of judicial decisions, to mandate taxpayer money to pay for capital improvements to a judge's liking?

Other judges impose their will by taking over the supervision of the school districts, as U.S. District Judge Ira DeMent did to the DeKalb County, Alabama public schools. In his 17-page order, again according to the Court Jester Awards, Judge DeMent ordered school employees to censor students' voluntary religious utterances, forced taxpayers to pay for persons to spy on their schools and report back to him, and mandated the distribution of a favorable interpretation of his ruling in order to support his position.

Another example of judicial activism comes from the bench of U.S. District Court Judge Harold Baer. In 1996 he excluded evidence after police witnessed men throwing heavy duffel bags into a van and fleeing upon approach by the police. The good judge claimed it was natural for drug dealers to run from police and thus this was not evidence of a crime in progress. No kidding!

Here's another example in which the *purpose* of government is subverted: Executive Orders. Few of us have heard of this presidential shortcut, and still fewer know what they really are.

According to attorney William J. Olson, editor of *Issues Bulletin*, there have been over 13,000 Executive Orders issued since George Washington's first proclamation to declare a National Day of Thanksgiving. Many of them, he contends, are invalid because they are not based upon the U.S. Constitution or other appropriate statutes. Only two executive orders in our history have been overturned as invalid by the U.S. courts, even though Congress has thirty days to review and vote them up or down by majority rule. He declares Congress, the courts and even the media have failed to pursue the constitutionality of Executive Orders.

Executive Orders are supposed to be issued to manage the operations of the government. Some constitutionalists see some Executive Orders as interfering with other branches of the government or states' sovereignty, and therefore are unconstitutional.

But even more frightening is that the President merely has to declare a State of National Emergency to exercise his emergency powers, even those powers which remain exclusively with the Congress. Most presidents have declared a National State of Emergency, but I'll bet you'll be as surprised as I was to learn that we have been under a National State of Emergency since March 1933, with this so-called emergency extended 13 times by President Clinton, who has issued over 200 Executive Orders.

Who knows why we are in a National State of Emergency today, but we are. Presently we have twelve active Executive Orders declaring a National State of Emergency for one reason or another.

For example, in 1994 President Clinton declared a National State of Emergency and issued an Executive Order for export controls. Later he declared another National State of Emergency for weapons of mass destruction. Still later, one on Bosnia-Herzegovina, and then Middle East terrorism, Colombian drug dealers, Cuba, Burma and the Sudan. It's hard to imagine that we are under siege and that the president of the United States has to declare a State of National Emergency.

It appears clear to me that his purpose, and perhaps that of other presidents as well, has been to declare national emergencies solely to enact Executive Orders without fear of congressional or court action.

Not since Abraham Lincoln have the courts overturned an Executive Order. What does that say about the role of Congress in this debate? In fact, did you know that your private boat could be seized by the government under the Merchant Marine Act of 1936, which authorized the requisition or purchase of any vessel or watercraft during any National Emergency? Isn't this a little out of control? Executive Orders, which interfere with other branches of the government, are bad enough, but what is the purpose of 12 active declarations of a National State of Emergency?

Another example in which the purpose of government has been perverted lies in the growth of regulatory agencies of the federal and state governments. These agencies have enormous oversight responsibilities and enormous powers. They regularly issue policy decisions that have a profound affect on the way the nation does business and those regulators are not accountable to the voter. They are appointees, not elected to the post, and they often work without oversight from Congress.

Executive Orders, legislation, and regulatory and judicial decisions all have an enormous and cumulative effect upon our daily lives. Fortunately, the pendulum is starting to swing towards efficiency. The government, although still massive and inefficient, is starting to change, particularly after the Republicans took control of the Congress and the statehouses. We may like the Gingrich revolution or we may not, but all of us can see the slow but sure dismantling of the welfare state (both at the federal and state level). Balanced budgets, formerly pushed only by conservatives, are now a part of the liberal agenda, as is campaign reform.

But we still need to keep asking ourselves, do we need all this governmental infrastructure and regulation? You decide, but first insist that we conduct a comprehensive review of the purpose for their existence, and then demand that Congress modify or delete them as warranted.

*"There can be no surer
sign of decay in a country
than to see the rites of religion
held in contempt."*
Niccolò Machievelli
1469-1527

Chapter 11: The Purpose of Religion

***The purpose of religion is to provide a moral fabric
for our lives.***

Several times a year, our nation collectively forgets
the rhetoric that so often displays its ugly head at any
mention of God. Only during Christmas and Hanukkah,
Easter, Thanksgiving and a few other religious holy days
do we invoke the word "God" without the sound and fury
coming from those who demand religion remain a private
matter.

But at any other time of the year, dare try invoking
the word of God in public or at a public institution and
face the consequences: a fearful outcry of distorted rhetoric
emanating from nonbelievers (and some fainthearted
believers) who stridently proclaim that the Constitution
demands that church and state remain separated.

I understand that many people in our society mistrust

the religious among us, particularly the faithful who try to foist their religion down our throats without regard to our own personal beliefs. Even among the many religious groups in America, passions flare when people are confronted about their own personal religion as compared to another.

However, one thing is clear to me. I sense that the majority of religious Americans—not the extremists who blow up abortion clinics in the name of saving babies, but the truly religious among us who are guided by their faith––possess an inner tranquility and serenity unmatched by those who do not share that same strength of spirit.

Call it hokey if you will, but those religious Americans who possess that inner peace tend to focus their lives on a higher purpose. They tend to focus on right versus wrong, truth versus falsehood, kindness versus cruelty. It's called common decency and a spirit of love and friendship that directs their lives to seek good over evil. Those who lack this basic moral compass, this inner serenity, are not focused on good versus evil; they see life simply as a matter of living day-to-day without a higher sense of purpose.

With regard to the Christmas season, I can understand why a business desires to put out nonsectarian holiday greetings or advertisements to be inclusive of all of their current or potential customers. But it isn't necessarily wrong for the general population, regardless of the Politically Correct Thought Police, to offer a genuinely sincere and heartfelt *Merry Christmas!* or *Happy Hanukkah!* to ordinary people you meet on the street or in a department store. But of course the PC Thought Police will call you insensitive because the person receiving the greeting may take offense. Well, excuse me, but a heartfelt religious greeting during the holidays should not be taken as an insult, after all it is meant in a holiday spirit, a spirit of goodwill.

Many seem to have forgotten that this nation was

founded on religious principles so dear to our ancestors that the Founding Fathers included religious language in every important and historic document in our archives. From the Constitution and the Bill of Rights to the Declaration of Independence and the Federalists' Papers, references to God, religion and the state are so intertwined as to be inseparable.

It doesn't make any sense to me to allow the invocation of God during religious seasons such as Christmas or Hanukkah, but at other times of the year it becomes strictly a private matter. Never mind that we combine church and state at many public and private functions every day of the year. On a daily basis we hear God's word at funerals and weddings and baptisms, many of which are conducted in public buildings and on public grounds around the nation. At military Changes of Command on government property, chaplains provide an invocation prior to the ceremony, and a benediction following the official change of command. A prayer from the House or Senate Chaplain precedes the opening of Congress. And even the Senate Impeachment trial of President Clinton began with a daily prayer in the U.S. Capitol. Where were the protestors for separation of church and state at these hearings? Perhaps they decided not to watch television. Or perhaps they see no harm in opening public hearings with a prayer to an adult Senate audience, but are still squeamish when it comes to opening a school day with prayer to a group of impressionable youngsters.

In any case, this intertwining of church and state occurs a lot more frequently than most people are aware. So why then do some people become so infuriated over the mention of God in public forums (except of course around the religious holidays)?

In my opinion this reaction is no more than another form of situational ethics! Some who are atheist or agnostic make misleading claims for their own personal agendas about the Founding Fathers' intent with the First Amendment. They do not have a clue as to the purpose that religion plays in the lives of most Americans, and they are dead wrong about the Founding Father's interpretation of the separation of church and state. Nonbelievers have tried to revise history by insisting the church never had any connection with the public arena. That is a dishonest review of our history. Our ancestors certainly didn't see it that way. At the time our nation was founded, only a minority of activists was concerned about the separation of church and state. For them, separation meant that the state (government) should not endorse any particular religion over another. However, during my lifetime, revisionists have interpreted the Establishment clause (separation of church and state) narrowly in order to forbid recognition of the existence of God in public institutions. That's a dishonest interpretation. Separation was not meant to discourage the right to freedom of speech or freedom of religion.

Quite often I hear repeated cries from the liberal left who claim that religion should be a private affair and that there is no room for it in public discourse. If that statement is true, then the opposite is also true; that there should be no denunciation in public of those who do believe that religion has its place in the heart of America. Talk about hypocrisy! It is hypocritical of those who stand for the rights of individuals to do what they think is best for them and their children and then to choose to ignore the religious individual's right to do what they think is best for their family, simply because the issue deals with religion.

Religious beliefs are entirely a personal matter between you and your God, but they are not necessarily a private affair. We cannot compartmentalize religious beliefs into separate categories depending upon our location. We would not expect an atheist to disavow God in public but endorse His teachings in private. It doesn't work that way. That is to say, you have an absolute right to disagree with my religious beliefs and speak out against them, but then don't be hypocritical and deny me the right to profess my faith.

Those who loudly profess their faith have become known as the Religious Right. They have been labeled as fanatics and extreme right wingers because they choose to make a stand publicly against immorality as they see it. They have that right; it's called the First Amendment. Because many members of the Religious Right disavow homosexuality as immoral behavior, they are branded as intolerant bigots. My guess is that most do not accept the practice of a homosexual life-style as moral, so they speak out against it; but that does not automatically equate to being intolerant.

Remember Free Speech? These people are merely expressing their views on morality and trying to change minds.

You have an equal right to disagree with their moralistic view. If you do, does that make you intolerant of their right to believe in a heterosexual life-style? Of course not! But you'd think that the media would get it right. Instead, they label one side as intolerant, even when both sides staunchly defend their position with equal (but opposite) logic, using the same Bill of Rights to make their points.

The modern, politically correct view is that we must accept and tolerate every aberration of moral behavior, or otherwise be labeled as intolerant and judgmental. That view of course is ridiculous. I do not have to accept immoral behavior, nor do I have to accept being called intolerant merely because I choose to defend morality. Tolerance does not mean I have to accept everything I disagree with! Conversely, because you disagree with me doesn't give you the right to claim that I am intolerant.

Similarly, opponents of the partial-birth abortion procedure, who vigorously attempt to persuade a mother to save her child, are labeled anti-choice, mean spirited and intolerant of the mother's rights. Proponents, on the other hand, who vigorously defend a mother's right to choose to have an abortion, are never labeled intolerant or mean spirited.

Why is that?

It reminds me of the Clinton impeachment trial in the Senate when all the Republicans (except four) voted to convict the President, and all of the Democrats voted to acquit. The Republicans were labeled partisan because all (but four) voted in bloc. But all of the Democrats also voted in bloc. So why weren't they labeled partisan? The answer of course is that there is a hidden agenda: the media has helped persuade the public that the liberal philosophy is the correct one. Thus, you are labeled partisan, or intolerant, or bigoted, or mean spirited if you are on the wrong side of the argument, according to the press.

Obviously we need to retrace our religious roots and study our history in order to understand the purpose that religion plays in our daily lives.

Intolerance has always been a label attached to extreme ideas—ideas that run contrary to mainstream thinking. In other words, if you do not think as the mainstream does, you must be intolerant of its ideas, rather than simply disagreeing with them. But this thinking begs another question: what is an extreme idea? Is it anything right of center, or just those extremely right of center? But isn't there left of center thinking and far left of center thinking also? Of course there is. So who decides what is mainstream and what is not? Do we take a poll? Do we allow the media (who have acknowledged that they are 80 to 85 percent liberal in their views) decide? Unfortunately, the press, academia and television have defined mainstream thinking for us for some time now, creating a public backlash that accounts for the huge popularity of conservative talk radio (Rush Limbaugh Show) and cable news programs (Fox News Channel)—shows which counter the liberal media in defining mainstream thinking and intolerance.

Intolerance goes both ways. Therefore, why are pro-lifers called extremists and intolerant while pro-choicers get a pass. Is it because a few who bomb abortion clinics claim to be pro-lifers that the rest are labeled extreme? Then why not include on the extremist list those who advocate and actually perform partial-birth abortions? To many, taking the life of a baby who is merely inches away from taking his first breath is an act of murder. It surely seems like an extreme act to me! Why doesn't the media label these so-called doctors extremists? Doesn't the media's own inaction reveal they are the ones who are intolerant?

I'm certainly not advocating bombing abortion clinics. That would be criminal behavior. But I do feel that those who speak out loudly against murdering babies (legalized abortion or not) have a constitutional right to speak and deserve not to be labeled by a liberal press as extremists for their views. It's this same press which has portrayed conservative talk radio as extremist thought. Why do they not understand that for millions and millions of Americans, conservative ideas are a philosophy of life; their views are no more extreme or intolerant of others than are those of liberals.

According to most accounts, Americans are a religious people who regularly attend church services. Many, if not most, contribute to charities sponsored by their churches or synagogues. Many send their children to private or parochial schools to ensure they receive a moral upbringing that is no longer evident in the public school systems. And many more, who cannot afford to send their children to private or parochial schools, have become increasingly frustrated with a public school system that disregards parental concerns regarding the lack of moral teaching in the school curriculum. If a few speak out, they are immediately labeled right wingers and intolerant. They cannot break through the administration or the teachers' unions to express their views on existing curriculums. Many are disgusted with the mandatory social and cultural diversity classes that have nothing to do with academic study. They are not bigots, they simply want to be assured that what their children are taught conforms to their moral beliefs. They don't necessarily want to include religious studies, but simply don't want subjects taught to their children that run counter to their beliefs.

Why is that labeled intolerant?

It seems to me that if you want to teach tolerance by introducing the homosexual life-style into the classroom, why can't you teach about different faith-based life-styles using the same argument? If you want to teach children how to use condoms to prevent AIDS, then why not teach them about abstinence which surely will prevent AIDS? If you consider mandatory cultural diversity teaching to be an endorsement by the government, surely then the lack of inclusion of faith-based teaching should be considered as a negative endorsement by the government.

Just where does the Constitution say it is okay to include amoral discussions in school curriculum, but not moral discussions? Here is what the Constitution does have to say on these matters—it's called the First Amendment: "Congress shall make no law respecting an establishment of religion, or prohibiting the free exercise thereof." That's pretty clear to me.

We can't have it both ways. Either provide a full discussion that includes all views, or honor the wishes of many devout religious parents not to teach subjects that inflame their passions on morality. Or even better yet, get back to the basics, and we won't have these fundamental arguments as to which social agendas to teach.

*"All who have meditated
on the art of governing man-
kind have been convinced that
the fate of empires depends on
the education of youth."*
Aristotle
384 - 322 B.C.

Chapter 12: The Purpose of Education

**The purpose of education is to prepare our youth
to become well informed, active citizens capable of
earning a living and performing their civic duties.**

Would you be shocked to learn that in many public
school systems throughout the country, students are
graduating without the ability to read and write at the
high school level? Would you believe that many who have
already been accepted for undergraduate education are
required to take summer school remedial courses because
they lack the basic vocabulary, writing and spelling skills?
Would you be outraged if you knew that for many of our
disadvantaged youths in the inner cities of America, the

129

word *education* is a misnomer?

What have we done to our public education system in this country?

For many, their public school career is little more than a mandatory check in the box to be promoted from grade to grade until graduation time, regardless of the basic skills they may or may not have learned. It is even difficult for many graduates to fill out a job application form accurately. There are some, of course, who will make it through with the help of their devoted parents and dedicated teachers, but for many students school has been little more than one long recess.

This is why many concerned parents either clamor for school vouchers, opt out of the public school system, or home-school their children themselves. Many prefer the discipline of private or parochial schools. Others prefer the physical safety not inherent in many of our local public schools.

I opted for parochial education for both of my children, despite the fact it cost me twice (public school taxation and private school admission). I realize that this was my own choice, and I don't regret it for one minute. But at least I had the choice because I could afford it. Most of the middle class and affluent members of society do exactly what I did if they live in a district where the public school systems are an absolute failure.

Consider Washington, D.C., where the President, the Vice President and many senior members of the Clinton Cabinet and members of Congress who live in Washington, D.C. also opted out of these failed schools. Many of the public school teachers send their own children to private or parochial schools in the District, Virginia or Maryland for similar reasons. In Boston, a 1995 study of public school teachers reported that 44.6 percent of the city's public school teachers had their own children in private schools; 36.2 percent in Chicago; and 50.3 percent in Jersey City, N. J., according to the opinion page in *The Washington Times*. As teachers, they understand the importance of a first rate education in an environment free from drugs and gangs and the threat of physical harm. They understand the purpose of education and have the mobility to move to another, safer school district, or have the affluence to pay for private schooling.

Many governors and city mayors understand that every citizen should have an opportunity for a first rate education, not just those who can afford private schools. Thus, many have supported efforts to provide some students a way out of their failed public schools through vouchers. If we concur that it is in the government's scope of responsibility to provide for the education of our children from kindergarten through 12th grade, why are some communities opposed to these efforts?

We clearly expect that education be conducted in safe schools with motivated teachers and appropriate curriculum that will provide the students with the best opportunity to go on to vocational or collegiate level studies, or to get an entry-level job. We don't need curriculum that is intended to teach our children anything other than the basic requirements.

The purpose of primary and secondary education is not to teach my child how to put on a condom or celebrate the diversity of homosexuality. It is not the purpose of the government (public) school to teach my child about feminism or affirmative action or any of the latest diversity teachings. Those subjects for children under eighteen should be left to parents, counselors, or clergy. Beyond that, it should be left to higher education (liberal arts, private or state colleges) to offer those kinds of subjects in their own curriculum. Grade schools and high schools, on the other hand, have mandatory curriculums, and therefore their subject areas should be in the best interest of all their students.

School boards need to rediscover the purpose for every curriculum they have approved in the past and to determine if they have met the purpose for which they sit in judgment.

How have we managed over the years to dumb down our education system? Since establishing the federal Department of Education, it seems that standards are set lower and lower, and students are learning less and less. What was right with our educational standards prior to the '70s that is not right today to warrant federal intervention of a local issue? Were our high school graduation rates or our scholastic aptitudes back then so great that it required no federal intervention, but they do today? Were the schools our grandparents and parents attended more responsive to their educational needs compared with today's standards? Wasn't there a mandatory federal requirement prior to 1970 as there is today, that every American child attends school? If that is the case, how has the addition of the federal Department of Education helped the student? Have graduation rates increased? Have our national scholastic aptitude results increased compared to worldwide figures?

Hardly.

Clearly, neither graduation nor scholastic aptitude rates have increased since the '70s What then, was the purpose in establishing the Department of Education?

In my opinion, we have simply bloated the government bureaucracy by adding thousands of employees at taxpayer expense. We've increased the workloads for school boards and school administrators by adding reams of red tape. We've thrown billions upon billions of dollars at school systems mandating innumerable new social curriculums that have absolutely nothing to do with learning the basic skills required to earn a living after graduation.

Disagree if you will, but the bottom line is that we have not improved our educational standards since the establishment of the Department of Education. We've added thousands of new positions at the federal, state and local level to comply with the red tape from Washington; we've decreased the average in-class teaching time; and we have a Department of Education that spends nationwide over $250 billion dollars a year to teach 52 million K-12 students, only to find ourselves well below the standards of our parents and grandparents generations.

It's time to do something about it for the sake of our nation's children!

Between 1970 and 1990, real U.S. education expenditures increased 80 percent while test scores stagnated, according to Anne H. Whittenbury, writing for the Josiah Bartlett Center for Public Policy. She claims there are many inefficiencies today which include a push to smaller classes, complying with expensive state and federal mandates of questionable benefits, bloated administrative structures, teacher tenure and the ever-increasing growth of intrusive nonacademic programs. Why, she asks, do Catholic schools typically spend one half to one third as much money per student as public schools, but repeatedly produce higher achievement scores (according to a five year experiment by the Annie E. Casey Foundation)? In addition, Anne Whittenbury insists that throwing money at the problem is not the solution. For example, New Hampshire spent $1.4 billion dollars to educate just under 200,000 students in K-12 ($7,300 per pupil) and ranked 15th in expenditures but 28th in SAT scores. On the other hand, Iowa ranked first in SAT scores, but 30th in expenditures per pupil.

Did you know that the Department of Education manages 244 education programs? In addition, another 30 other federal agencies administer 308 more educational programs. Imagine the taxes saved if we rid ourselves of this behemoth bureaucracy that apparently serves no purpose in improving our educational standards.

In Martin Gross' book entitled, *The Conspiracy of Ignorance: The Failure of American Public Schools,* he has recorded a shocking testimony of the failure of American public schooling compared to other nations. He cites a 63-question exam where sixty percent of American 8th-graders from 200 schools failed in this simple math question. What is the average age of five children aged 13, 8, 6, 4 and 4? The Americans came in dead last among the Koreans, Spanish, British, Irish and four provinces which participated from Canada. Naturally, the Americans came in first in "self-esteem" when asked to check yes or no to the statement: I am good at math.

Even more shocking, according to *The Washington Times*, was the failure of our teachers. Of 1,800 education graduates seeking teachers' licenses in Massachusetts, 59 percent flunked the screening test.

Some may wonder how we maintain our technological edge in the face of the failure of our public schools. The answer is also shocking.

Martin Gross reports that some 45 percent of the 13,000 hard science Ph.D.'s in America today are awarded each year to non-Americans!

Despite this failure, the cost to educate our children has risen twice as fast as inflation over the past 30 years and has produced little in the way of academic excellence.

Education in America has historically been a state issue, not a federal issue. Why then did federal appeals court Judge Solomon Oliver Jr. temporarily strike down, on the eve of classes commencing in the city of Cleveland, a three-year-old program to let low income families send their kids to private or suburban schools. Judge Oliver, according to syndicated columnist Tony Snow, having three years to determine the constitutionality of this program, ruled on the last day before the start of a new school year, that because 85 percent of the students attended sectarian institutions, this program was unconstitutional.

What was the purpose of announcing his ruling on the day before classes started? He certainly didn't have the best interest of the children in mind when he made his ruling.

Because of the timing of his announcement, I believe he was touting his own personal agenda at the expense of those children. The clamor that followed forced him to rethink his decision so that at least the children could attend school while the decision was worked out.

George W. Bush's recent proposal to withhold federal dollars from failed public schools makes sense. Why throw money at an inept school administration? Let's give the kids in those schools the education they deserve.

It's not fair that the government makes it mandatory for children to go to the public school within the district they live if their school administrators and teachers are failing them, and then not give them the same opportunity to learn as other children who happen to live in another public school district.

For a change, let's not get bogged down in the inevitable and endless debate of state versus church, or draining public schools of taxpayer dollars, but instead truly think of the children. You know what, I'll bet the children don't care; it's the teachers' unions and the parents who squawk.

If given a choice, would you send your child to a school that has failed to live up to its standards, or to a school that has exceeded those standards? If your purpose as a parent is to provide the best for your child, then there really is only one answer.

Education is a lifelong pursuit for many. Successful people clamor to continue their education. Successful businesses recognize the need to hire the brightest people and provide them with the requisite training to ensure they can compete in the marketplace. Seminars, training courses, briefings and adult education classes all are designed for the same purpose in order to improve the participant's level of knowledge on a particular subject. Community colleges, universities and graduate level studies abound for the same reason.

The key to success in America, however, is to recognize how to successfully communicate, orally and verbally, in the use of the English language, no matter the undertaking. It is the key to promotion, an increased paycheck and an improved standard of living. However, some disagree with the importance of teaching the English language. They believe education ought to be taught in the native tongue or dialect of the student. That thinking may lead to a student's graduation certificate, but it is not necessarily the means for improving their standard of living.

When I was in school, almost every semester we had to take an English class. More than math or science, English studies provided the majority of our class assignments. Reading, writing and arithmetic were viewed as important subjects to master, and many School Boards and principals understood that communication was the necessary ingredient to become successful in life.

Recently, however, a West Virginia University assistant professor opined on a Fox News Channel, that we need not have standards for the use of the English language because that portends a bias towards certain dialects. He is encouraging his students to submit assignments without regard to the correct use of English composition, vocabulary, sentence structure, context, spelling and the like, and suggesting Ebonics (which is not a dialect) and other incorrect uses of the English language is fashionable in his class. He declares that this is in fact good for his students to observe and learn from other cultures.

Now keep in mind, this is a university professor. I don't know what his contract requires him to teach, but I doubt that he is teaching his students the correct use of the English language. It appears, according to his comments, that he is merely collecting assignments without judging their composition, as is his responsibility to do as an English professor. His students will be shortchanged in the end. Is he truly fulfilling his purpose? Or does he have an agenda to push at the expense of his students?

Many educators, sociologists and psychologists over the past few decades have pushed the notion that we should not discipline bad behavior in school or correct poor performance in the classroom for fear of hurting a person's feelings or making a value judgment that stigmatizes the student. They suggest discipline and correction only instill anger, resentment, jealousy and revenge. They prefer to "talk about" their feelings rather than provide and enforce a standard to meet. They suggest that a person's personal beliefs cannot be ignored and should not be judged against a societal standard, particularly one established by "white males". They don't understand that in the real world, not in the world of academia, discipline and performance standards are the norm.

Why do they continue to promote this rubbish?

This type of thinking has caused the greatest divide

among members of my generation who were taught to meet certain standards to be successful in life; versus a new generation of young people who have little to no conception that standards provide an order to life, a challenge to meet. Many young people today feel as if they should not be denied anything based upon their own personal point of view. This thinking has led to ill-advised discrimination lawsuits because many people "feel" entitled to the right to do anything they want.

Therefore, let's insist that our schools return to teaching the basics. Let's make English studies the linchpin of our education system and demand minimum standards to graduate.

"Military force—especially when wielded by an outside power—cannot bring order in a country that cannot govern itself."
Robert McNamara, 1995

Chapter 13: The Purpose of the Military

The purpose of the military is to provide for the training, equipment and logistical support of the Armed Forces, for the common defense of our national interests.

Our country has a strong military tradition, with a civilian-controlled military establishment as old as the nation itself. Our first president was our first general. The Secretary of Defense ranks only behind the Secretaries of State and Treasury in order of precedence and seniority.

Those uniformed service personnel and civilians who make up the forces of the Army, Navy, Marine Corps, Air Force and Coast Guard represent the United States military

as we know it today.   They are divided among the
Departments of Defense and Transportation (U.S. Coast
Guard).

They exist for the purpose of defending our national
interests at home and abroad. This much is clear.

But who defines those national interests? The press?
The public? Congress? The President? The Constitution,
for better of for worse, is pretty vague at this point, leaving
the President basically in charge as Commander-in-Chief.

The national security team headed by the
Commander-in-Chief has at times successfully justified
our military excursions to Congress and to our allies. At
other times the President has introduced our troops into
foreign lands based upon executive branch "political"
diplomacy, without full consultation, advice or consent
from Congress or the American public.

Over the years we have lowered the size and changed
the makeup of our military branches and their units, and
we have redefined their missions. Yet depending upon
whose spin you believe and whose history you read, during
those years these missions have been as successful as not
in accomplishing our interpretation of defending our
national interests.

One thing certain is that the pace has picked up.

We have increasingly sent our young men (and women)
all over the globe to do battle in wars, conflicts, campaigns
or other so called "peacekeeping" missions. Their stated
purpose was to support our national interest.

Yes, we've sent our troops into harm's way for various
justifiable reasons, but I would argue that those reasons
in many instances were not specifically for the purpose of
defending our national interest.

Although the purpose of the military's very existence
has been clearly stated from the early days of our Republic,
I will suggest to you that the purpose of their deployment

has changed dramatically from one administration to another. The political environment and philosophical debate at the time has often left our national interests in the dust.

What then are our national interests? How should we use our military forces in support of them?

There is no easy answer to these questions because they provoke a debate that depends upon your philosophical viewpoint and the side of the political spectrum upon which you reside.

Those among us who are isolationists believe we should never use American forces other than to defend our soil against invasion. They see no reason whatsoever to use troops outside the United States territory regardless of our existing treaty obligations.

Others, who have a claim to humanitarianism, believe it is America's moral obligation to be the "world's policeman" in order to stop the killing, starving and ethnic cleansing of the world's minority populations.

Others, who might not be isolationists, find it difficult to send American troops abroad to possibly die, when we have no stated political objective, military goal, or timetable and exit strategy. They see no benefit to the mission and only a drain on our national resources, including the loss of valuable young American lives.

If Vietnam taught us nothing else, it taught us this: we should expect our leaders to accurately and honestly define for us just what the national interest is that we will be defending when we send our military forces into foreign conflicts. For after all, it will be our national resolve that will decide whether we will win the fight over the long haul.

It's hard to forget Vietnam, and few veterans and civilians of that era do.

After years of fighting with no end in sight, no military

objectives met, and the visibility of thousands of body bags arriving back home, American resolve among the populace and Congress eroded and protests increased throughout the nation. As American servicemen and women returned home they were welcomed with protests and chants and spit on their uniforms for dedicating their lives to their country, regardless of whether they personally believed in the purpose of the war.

We—soldiers and civilians alike—began to see that there was no purpose in continuing what we were doing. It became clear that we did not really intend to support an all out effort to free the South Vietnamese people from their northern aggressors. It had become obvious that our military was not going to be allowed to fully prosecute the war. Our "national will" had eroded, as illustrated by our failure to bomb or invade North Vietnam with any purpose of making them believe we were determined to win at all costs.

It is an undisputed fact that our military was not allowed "to win" in Southeast Asia. This was a political war run by the Executive Branch. With all the firepower and air superiority America had in the '60s, compared with the arms supplied by the Russians and Chinese to the North Vietnamese Army and the Viet Cong, the American military could have and should have won the war. United Nations Peacekeepers (in the true sense of the word) may have been in place today, as they are in South Korea, if America had persevered in Vietnam to stop the spread of communism.

But we lost the war, because we had no military objective, no achievable definition of "winning," no timetable, no exit strategy and little national resolve.

Regardless of whether our fighting in Vietnam was in our national interest—a debate that most military members had no control over anyway—the purpose of the military's mission during that war should not have changed. The purpose of the military intervention was to defend the South Vietnamese populace from domination by their northern neighbors.

We failed miserably, because we lost track of our purpose.

Should we have been isolationists or humanitarians? Should we have worried about the Cold War threat of communism spreading throughout the Third World countries? You decide.

But I can unequivocally state that during my tour of duty, flying helicopter gunships for the Navy in support of the Riverine forces and Navy SEALS in the Mekong Delta, I flew under rules that were self-defeating (not to mention *dangerous*). I was not allowed to shoot at certain targets in our area of operation, without first receiving prior permission to fire, even if being fired upon. The reason often given us was to prevent us from hitting friendly forces. But in actuality no friendly forces would be shooting at their own helicopters in the first place.

These rules were a cop out. Those of us on the firing line had our hands tied.

What a way to fight a war. No wonder we lost it.

Since then our American military forces have been engaged in many other locations around the world, allegedly defending our national interests in Grenada, the Persian Gulf, Somalia, Haiti, Bosnia, and Kosovo. President Reagan sent forces to the tiny island of Grenada to defend American medical students from the threat of communists. It worked.

President Bush dispatched American troops to Kuwait with Congressional, allied and Middle East support, after Saddam Hussein invaded it. America and its allies won decisively (although some will say we didn't go far enough) and the Kuwaitis were freed.

President Clinton sent humanitarian forces to help the starving people of Somalia, and quickly withdrew them after eighteen soldiers were killed. He also sent American peacekeeping forces into Haiti to help prop up the local presidential election, and into Bosnia-Herzegovina to keep the peace between Bosnians, Croats and Muslims. He has ordered American pilots to drop bombs and missiles on Yugoslavia to defend the Albanians in Kosovo from the ethnic cleansing by Slobodon Milosevic and his Serbian army.

Again, I ask, were all of these military actions in our national interest? Do we define our national interest and the use of our military in supporting it only in regard to protecting us from an enemy invading our soil? Would we be inclined to use the military in areas of the world if our standard of living was affected by world oil, textile or food prices?

Do we feel that Americans are obligated to send in the military to defend human rights around the world where freedoms are restricted by dictatorial regimes, or where centuries-old ethnic violence or religious hatred are causing civil unrest, death and destruction?

National interests, to my mind, need to be national in scope. Before sending in the troops, our national interests need to be outlined as part of a clear foreign policy with a stated purpose and intent for the use of American armed forces. Any American military mission on foreign soil needs to truly have the full support of Congress and the American people.

A foreign policy using the military for peacekeeping and humanitarian missions is not in keeping with the intended purpose for the use of our armed forces. American foreign policy should never be based upon a military intervention designed to support internal affairs, regardless of religious affiliations, national origins, or our own political emotions at the time.

We have been there, done that. It wasn't pretty.

This is why, as much as I dislike the fighting in Northern Ireland, I clearly believe the violence there is a local issue for the British and the Irish to contend with. Similarly in Yugoslavia.

Why did we try to resolve the peace in Bosnia with military force but not in Northern Ireland? Both countries have a legacy of centuries-old religious hatred among neighbors. Why should the United States choose between Protestants and Catholics, or among Bosnians, Croats and Muslims? Why do we need to broker their peace?

Across the globe these questions pop out. Why should we use our military in supporting regimes that are starving their own people; or waging ethnic war to displace peoples of other tribes, religions or ethnicity in their own countries? Why defend the starving in Somalia but not the starving in Rwanda? Why not invade China and defend the repressed students at Tiananmen Square who were seeking freedom and democracy, as we attempted to do with the ethnic Albanians seeking independence in Kosovo?

In my opinion, we should be using our military forces to defend our freedoms, both domestically and abroad, with clearly defined military objectives, mission and exit strategy. Never again should we encounter another Vietnam where we lacked the "will to win."

If we use the military correctly, we should make available our entire arsenal (short of nuclear weapons) to destroy the enemy or not dispatch them at all. Ever heard of trying to win a football game only using the pass (aerial bomb) and not using the run (ground attack)? Of course not! Therefore, I don't understand the logic that says, "Deploy the military, but don't bomb this building or that facility, and for heaven's sake, don't send in the ground troops."

What kind of strategy or logical thinking is that?

War is hell, but if we have already decided to conduct one, we'd better be prepared to finish it.

The problem with the Clinton administration is that they want to appear strong in deploying American military might, but they also want to appear sensitive in not hurting civilians.

But sometimes civilians get killed. It's the nature of war.

Many civilians died in World War II, but we didn't hesitate to win it.

Some matters of military intervention are a legal issue. We should intervene where we have entered legally into treaty obligations to defend other nations, such as NATO countries.

Kosovo is not a member nation of NATO and therefore does not meet the purpose of the defense treaty, despite the administration's insistence that this is a NATO conflict. Am I to believe that all the NATO countries don't understand the purpose of the defense treaty their own governments signed?

Of course, we should intervene if access to the world's oil and food markets or precious metals and mineral rights are threatened to the point that our way of life or that of our democratic partners is at risk.

We should intervene in foreign lands to defend our embassy personnel and other Americans living abroad; and in countries requesting our support when it clearly meets our national interest.

With clearly defined national interests as a backdrop for our military intervention, with the full support (or at least a clear majority) of the American people, we won't get into the arguments that reflect double standards of national policy such as defending Europeans against ethnic cleansing but not Africans; or providing humanitarian support for the starving in Somalia but not the starving in Sudan; or for providing military support to defend the government of Haiti but not for the freedom fighters in Tiananmen Square.

Because the taxpayers foot the bill, not the government, the President owes it to the American people to clearly make a case for military intervention. Unwise military incursions into foreign lands have in recent years created a financial drain that is depleting the resources of the American military.

Tanks, missiles, ships, aircraft, personnel and all of their supporting logistical pipelines are extremely expensive to operate. They are already sorely in need of modernization and upgrading. Military pay scales have not kept pace with the civilian sector. Because money to address these issues has been siphoned off to pay for bombs and cruise missiles dropped over Iraq and Serbia, morale has plummeted and the troops are leaving in droves.

Consider that the Army has lost eight of its eighteen divisions since the buildup for the Gulf War just ten years ago. The Air Force is flying aging aircraft, down from 79 squadrons to 52 today. The Navy's active fleet of battle forces to cover the world's oceans and hot spots is down over 160 combat ships; nuclear subs are down from 43 to 18; and other support ships from 106 to 50. Navy fighter and attack aircraft are down from 67 squadrons to 36 squadrons.

It's fair to ask if we need the same levels of forces for the 21st century as we did at the end of the Cold War. Perhaps we do not. But we must maintain what forces we have. We must equip them properly and provide our fighting men and women with the best training available. This requires money and resolve.

As long as we truly understand the purpose of the military—to defend our national interests—there is no doubt of the outcome.

Chapter 14: The Purpose of Taxation

The purpose of taxation is to cause private individuals and businesses to pay their fair share of public services which provide for the common good.

Do we really need to pay taxes? The answer is *yes*, if we expect the government to provide the necessary services that we demand. The problem, of course, is defining these necessary services.

Are all the federal, state and local taxes the average American pays really necessary? I contend they are not.

I also contend that if we were to cut the percentage of our total taxes in half (at all levels), the general population would be for the most part unaware of the programs that would be eliminated or reduced because of the lack of funding.

We would hear the distorted rhetoric emanating from the mouths of those special interest groups affected by the loss of tax revenues to support their pet projects, but the ordinary, average American would see only an increase in his or her paycheck. If this tax reduction eliminated Radio Marti, the National Endowment of the Arts, or the Tennessee Valley Authority funding, would we really care?

Of course we can justify the need to continue to pay for free national radio broadcasts to Cuba and other Central and South American countries, but we need to examine our accomplishments there. If we disband the National Endowment for the Arts, have we really stifled the encouragement for art in our society? What was the original purpose for establishing the Tennessee Valley Authority, and have we not accomplished that goal long ago?

Our U.S. and state representatives need to be asking themselves these questions on our behalf. However, they are loath to say "no" when "no" might mean eliminating jobs in their communities. Perhaps term limits *is* a good idea after all, to ensure that each representative remains a citizen-legislator rather than a legislator-citizen (like Bill Clinton, who has held public office practically his entire adult life). At least then there would be less pressure to seek continued political support at the expense of unbiased analysis of our totally out of control tax burden.

Even worse than the attitudes of our elected representatives, we seldom ask where our tax dollars actually go. Apparently we don't care. We simply complain, but we don't demand an accounting. Did you know that

Vice President Al Gore last year nearly doubled the taxes we pay for the Internet? The Federal Communications Commission (nonelected bureaucrats) imposed a $1.3 billion dollar annual tax on phone companies to help wire our schools to the Internet. By executive fiat, the Vice-President nearly doubled that figure ($2.25 billion) without the consent of Congress. The Constitution clearly requires that all revenue-raising bills originate in the House of Representatives.

In other words, there is no "legal controlling authority" for the Executive branch either to impose or to raise taxes, but it did, despite the complaints from some consumers who understand the governmental procedures for taxation.

For some reason, we haven't been persistent or loud enough in our demands for a long-overdue overhaul of the tax code. Our current tax structure punishes success with progressive taxes.

According to the IRS, the top one percent of wage earners pay 30 percent of the tax burden; the top five percent pay 50 percent; and the bottom 50 percent pay only five percent of all taxes. Demanding our politicians cut the taxation rate in half would provide two benefits. First, it would increase our current net take-home pay, and secondly it would force the bureaucrats who manage our public money to reevaluate the purpose of their programs.

Ask yourself what services you truly desire from the government. Remember that the average American taxpayer today pays more in taxes than he does to feed, shelter and clothe himself and his family combined. Is that fair? Is it fair that we work approximately four and a half months of the year just to pay taxes to a bloated government bureaucracy? Why is it we provide about 40 percent of our income to finance federal, state and local projects of which we know nothing about? Does Washington, D.C. or your state capital, the county seat or your city council really need to spend that much for public projects and programs? Are all those services needed, or are some of them simply desired?

According to the Congressional Budget Office, the readjusted fiscal year 1999 revenues will be up sixty-five percent from what was projected just seven years ago in 1992. The CBO also claims that federal taxes as a percentage of total economic output are at record levels. In fact, budget surpluses are projected (before the Kosovo bombing last year) to be nearly one trillion ($934 billion) dollars over the next five years, $2.6 trillion over the next ten years.

Tell me why the taxpayers should not get a tax cut to return some of their money? Why should we continue to provide monies to these government programs, when most of them do not affect our daily lives?

The 1998 H & R Block Income Tax Guide numbered 574 pages. This guide was written to help the taxpayer fill out his tax returns, but according to the Money Magazine annual experiment, 45 tax professionals gave 45 different answers, and fewer than one in four came within $1,000 of the correct answer.

What then, is the *purpose* of our tax code? George Will argues that our tax code kills family businesses by taxing estates as much as 70 percent, leaving the heirs without operating and improvement capitol to continue the business. Was that one of its intended purposes?

But back to the question. Which services should the federal government provide? As a nation we need a military to provide for the common defense. We probably need national parks and national cemeteries, national museums and national highways. We also probably need the Federal Reserve Board and national institutions for medical research; the Departments of Defense, State, Treasury; the Veterans Administration, NASA and any other federal agency that solely provides services that only the federal government can provide.

But do we really need to fund AmeriCorps? Why is the national government involved in offering jobs to a select group of people? You and I are paying for this program by providing funding from taxes to pay salaries for all involved. What is its purpose? What about funding the Peace Corps? Or funding the National Endowment for the Arts? Or funding the huge infrastructure associated with the Departments of Education, Commerce, Labor and Housing and Urban Development?

Are these really national priorities? Can we eliminate some or all of these bureaucracies, or perhaps combine some of their functions?

You bet we can!

My guess is that the majority of Americans cannot list the number, name or function of each of our Cabinet level departments. Do we need national policy on education, commerce, labor and housing? Of course we do! But we don't need an entire bureaucracy to support policies that are clearly local in nature or affect only a minority group of activists who have been successful in lobbying the government? Are we paying for their particular agendas? YOU BET WE ARE!

State, county and city government have similar bureaucracies that do not necessarily provide services to the majority of their constituents. Yes we need fire and police departments, the public demands it and it is clearly a local issue for the entire populace. We clearly demand other services, from recreation and parks to water, sewer and electric utilities. But have you ever looked up the number of governmental offices in the special pages of your local phone book? I'll bet you will be surprised at both the number and the titles listed. And I'll bet there are some offices you didn't even know existed. Just what are their functions? And how do we pay for all these services? Well, we pay state and federal income tax, sales tax, property tax, luxury tax, local option taxes, economic development taxes, restaurant and hotel taxes, estate taxes, capital gains taxes, cigarette and liquor taxes, and many other special use taxes such as hunting licenses, driver's licenses, fishing licenses, boating licenses, park entrance fees, you name it.

Don't misread me, there are many governmental functions that we clearly demand and that affect all of us. They need to remain. In addition, there are many other functions, such as licensing, that only affect a portion of the populace, but we clearly demand that they be funded by those who use the service.

Supposedly, in many states, these taxes on hunting, fishing and other recreational entertainment are designed to cover the cost of licensing and enforcement. So ask yourself why you pay for a boating license. What is the *purpose* for the government to require a license for your boat? Why does the government tax the gasoline for the boat, while it also makes you pay a property tax on it each year?

There may be valid reasons. The taxes may help pay for cleanup of the river or provide public boat ramps to launch your boat. My guess, however, is that we don't know where that money goes or what it actually funds.

As long as we agree that we need to license people to operate or recreate, then it is appropriate to pay the tax to cover the administration and enforcement costs. But that is the issue. We need to ensure that the cost to cover the expenses is appropriate and not excessive. Therefore, the need to constantly review the purpose of the agency is important to determine its relevance.

Has the bureaucracy grown too big? Has the original intent changed to encompass other functions? Are those other local functions germane, if county and city agencies and commissions duplicate the efforts of state or federal agencies?

Many will claim that to institute state and federal mandates requires similar functions within the county or city government just to manage the paperwork. But there are other choices. Rather than burdening the existing staff with additional responsibilities, the services can be contracted or additional people hired to man the new office. In any case, a new mandate is not cost free.

I recall in the Navy when higher authority mandated a new program for providing foreign area officer expertise to embassy, consulate and defense cooperation offices. We were told to support this new initiative with existing manpower, although it necessarily required the coordination of many offices on the major staffs around the world to make it work.

But that is precisely the problem I have been talking about.

In the Navy, our new headquarters program required the various echelon commands comply with the new mandate. I'm not suggesting it was a bad idea, but rather it was not cost free, and by its nature, it was more layered government. And layered government requires additional taxes to support its infrastructure; and additional infrastructure requires justification to fund it; and bureaucrats who think up new ideas can always justify their programs in the name of saving money in the long run by increased efficiency.

But a funny thing happens: these new programs, with their highly touted new efficiencies, continually grow and grow and grow and require additional monies to cover the cost of additional workers, new office spaces, and of course the cost of living adjustment.

It's a never-ending cycle.

"Children are our most valuable natural resource."
Herbert Hoover

Chapter 15: The Purpose of Parenting

The purpose of parenting is to nurture and protect our children and to instill in them the principles of right and wrong so that they may become good neighbors and solid, upstanding citizens.

Why do we have children? I think I know, having raised two myself.

But I wonder how many of us think that bringing children into the world is little more than a mistake of some nighttime extracurricular activity. In some cases, if that mistake gets in our way, it's no big deal. That's why we have abortions or adoptions or foster care, anything that relieves us of our responsibility as a parent.

My wife and I value our children. They were wanted, adored, nurtured and loved from the moment my wife knew she was pregnant. Even today, with a son who turned twenty-one last year and a daughter off to college in a couple of years, they are still our children. We will cherish every moment with them for the rest of our lives.

But there are others who don't share this attitude. In fact, many men today deny their children's existence, even to the point of not paying child support. "Deadbeat dads" they are called.

Some use the lame excuse that they have other lives to live now and new families to care for. These men have forgotten (or never knew) what it means to be a parent. They have forgotten the original purpose behind the court's decision to order child support payments.

So they whine and blame society for their own lack of responsibility towards their children. But in fact, they have abandoned their responsibilities, as have mothers who abandon their babies to abortion, adoption or foster care.

Why do so many men and women feel little emotion for their newborn child? How can they have no connection with a baby they have just nurtured through nine months of pregnancy? Why do some show no shame for terminating the life of a viable fetus?

I'm at a loss to explain what can only be described as a selfish act to defend their personal freedom over their sense of responsibility to a helpless baby who did not ask to be abandoned, or worse, aborted.

Over the past thirty and more years since the '60s, a generation of free love and free sex began its domination of our society's norms. A cycle of social despair has evolved that has generated social ills even more devastating than premarital sex and dead beat dads. This despair has been so destructive to the moral character of the American psyche that it has now affected many aspects of our daily lives, from latchkey kids and an abundance of poorly staffed day care centers, to uncaring nannies and baby sitters, to doctors who perform abortions even after swearing to the Hippocratic Oath.

This obsession with personal freedom has left an ugly scar on our conscience with regard to our personal responsibilities as parents. Daily we dump our toddlers off at day care centers, completely ignoring the *purpose* of parenting.

We have confused parenting with earning a living.

We have shirked our responsibility when we allow our preteens and teenagers to succumb to the whims of their own misbehavior and curiosity when they are allowed to be latchkey kids without supervision.

And we have permanently altered the reputation of life-preserving medicine when unscrupulous doctors conduct abortions on healthy babies and fetuses. Particularly gruesome is the partial-birth abortion where all but the head of the baby is delivered, and then pierced with a tool so that the brains can be vacuumed out.

What does the Hippocratic Oath mean to doctors who perform these kinds of unwarranted abortions? They claim to provide services in a safe environment so those desperate women don't seek abortions in back-alley, unclean facilities.

In reality, these doctors are supporting the irresponsible actions of confused women who have no conscience and who don't know what it means to be a parent.

What is the purpose of the Hippocratic Oath, which was meant to save lives, if doctors don't abide by it?

Regardless of the fact that in America today it is perfectly legal to perform partial-birth abortions, it doesn't make it right. It certainly begs the question, "What is the purpose in taking the Hippocratic Oath"? If I were a doctor today, I would stand on principle as many doctors in our country do, regardless of the consequences, and take my oath seriously. Otherwise, why have this oath? If it is outmoded, do away with it. Or perhaps the American Medical Association would like to ask its membership to reevaluate the meaning that they see in taking their sacred, historic oath.

I wonder what the AMA would discover. Their answer affects whether the current oath needs to be kept, or if it should be modified to serve a new purpose, which obviously includes the killing of unborn children.

Parenting isn't simply bearing children, feeding and clothing them, and then sending them out the door to school or day care. No, parenting is a full time job requiring all the coping skills imaginable. It is hard work; it is demanding and it isn't easy.

Families which prefer the satisfaction of two working paychecks are often doing so for purposes other than nurturing their children. "Day Care can adequately take care of my child's needs, because I need to earn that extra money for that big screen TV, or my bass fishing boat, or the latest computer software," those families seem to be saying.

I'm not impugning two-working-parent families. Some need to work two jobs in order to send their children to private schools to escape the failed public schools in their area and others need it just to make ends meet.

I'm suggesting rather, that we reevaluate our needs. Are we working that second job for the right reasons? Are we working for our personal satisfaction or for our children's needs? Who should come first?

Whatever you decide, that's your personal business, but let's understand the *purpose* of having children in the first place, rather than trying to justify why we need that second job. Be honest with yourself and your children. Is this a choice about good parenting? Or is it simply a choice for a more extravagant life-style? The true answer might hurt.

We need to remember that it is also our responsibility as a parent (for a lifetime) to ensure the mental, moral and physical well being of our children. We need to protect them from their own unintentional curiosity and peer pressure. We need to provide them discipline and show them love.

We don't need to leave to others an honest discussion of sex, drugs and gang behavior. We need to act as role models to re-enforce reality between our words and our actions. We need to be consistent and fair and show them the purpose of their actions.

It's time to challenge the silly notion that it takes a village to raise our children. That's ridiculous. The hidden meaning is that if I don't take my parenting responsibilities seriously, well then the village (government) will help me. But at what cost?

Will the so-called village—thinly disguised as government social programs—provide the moral teachings that I think are appropriate? I think not!

Think about the abrogation of parental responsibility over the past 20 or 30 years. We've allowed day care centers and preschools to provide the discipline and love (or lack of them) that is so necessary during our children's formative years.

We've allowed the public school systems and its liberal social curriculums to foster curiosity about sex, drugs and tolerance to amoral behavior, which run counter to many

of our religious beliefs. And we've allowed the personal
life-style or sexual proclivities of the health or gym teachers
to describe the do's and don'ts of private, intimate sexual
behavior to our impressionable teenagers, without regard
for parental concerns.

Yet, because of the liberals' interpretation of the
separation of church and state clause of the Constitution,
we introduce no moral interpretation of these issues, nor
are we allowed to make judgment of their consequences.

Value systems, say the schools, are not our
responsibility. Parents are responsible for their children's
discipline and behavior. Yet, we expect the school or the
teacher or the coach to handle the misbehavior that
inevitably occurs with kids who sense no love or caring or
individual attention from their parents.

Some parents have abrogated their responsibilities for
the sake of personal freedom. Then they complain mightily
that the schools are not doing enough to raise their children
properly.

We fill our children's heads full of self-esteem and "feel
good" emotions, so that we don't hurt their feelings. We'd
rather talk to our children than discipline them. We'd
rather be their buddies than their parents.

Our children are looking for guidance and the two
most important people in the world to them are often too
busy to care, or have abandoned them for their own
personal reasons.

No, it doesn't take a village to raise a child; it takes
two loving, responsible parents who care and understand
the purpose of parenting.

It's not an easy task to raise children today. There
are so many distractions that can occupy their attention:
drugs, alcohol, sex, the Internet, video games, MTV and
other television, and movies. But that doesn't mean

parenting today is any harder than yesterday.

Parenting is not a priority with many of today's parents because of all the distractions that occupy Mom's and Dad's attention. With the exception of new technology video games and the Internet, my parents' generation had just as many distractions, but quite clearly the distractions were less destructive ones. My parents worried about me smoking cigarettes; I worry about my kids smoking marijuana or using hard drugs. My parents worried about me getting into a fistfight; I worry about my kids getting caught in the middle of a shoot-out.

Clearly the consequences are different, but the challenges for parents remain the same.

Children throughout the ages have imitated their parents. But it is not the children today who have given up; it's the parents.

It's the parents who have decided to divorce at alarming rates, leaving children bereft of a father figure. It's the parents who have decided to work two jobs just to buy the latest technology-driven toy, leaving their children to fend for themselves for most of the day.

It's the parents, who in search of their personal freedom, have allowed the school systems to dictate the Cultural Revolution curriculum that lacks any mention of moral values. And it's the parents who have neglected to teach their children about morals and ethics and principles and values, a failure that has allowed the decay of civility among our youth to escalate into violence.

With prosperity at record highs and new technology providing us with labor saving devices and expensive adult toys with which to entertain ourselves, parents have opted for two jobs so that they can have it all.

But in doing so, their selfishness has perhaps caused a social tragedy unparalleled in American society in the last half of the 20th century.

To fix the problem will take several generations, much longer than the rebuilding effort after the Great Depression or the World Wars. Human nature requires more than money and a construction plan to rebuild; it requires purpose and the dedicated effort of millions of parents who don't like what they currently see in our national morality.

*"No athlete is crowned
but in the sweat of his brow."*
Saint Jerome
342 - 420

Chapter 16: The Purpose of Sports

***The purpose of sports is to provide an atmosphere
of competition within a set form and body of rules
that instill discipline, a work ethic, teamwork,
sportsmanship, entertainment and grace under fire.***

Americans truly enjoy watching or playing sports; it
is valuable entertainment for us. We all enjoy rooting for
our favorite teams and watching our kids perform like a
junior Michael Jordan, Mark McGwire, Tiger Woods or
Lindsey Davenport. We often obsess, particularly we men,
over a loss to a team we thought we should have beaten,
or over the lack of sustained effort on the part of highly

165

paid athletes. We enjoy "dissing" the umpires, referees and other officials as a way to vent our frustrations and anxieties over the progress of the game. Sometimes we are simply trying to be funny for the other "fanatic" fans.

I'll admit that I did my fair share of jumping on the umpires and referees at my son's baseball and basketball games before he went off to college. Some may label my antics as uncivil behavior. But I assure you that I never used profanity or racist remarks, and I always directed my remarks towards the officials and never towards the kids. I don't mention this to receive your approval, but to demonstrate that many sports fanatics like myself have probably taken our unconditional love for the game a little too far at times.

When I was a child, sportsmanship was a big deal. Everyone—fans, parents and coaches alike—emphasized its virtue. In today's environment, with the "win at all costs" attitude and the "in your face" advertising that dominates today's media, sportsmanship is no longer considered an integral part of the game. This is unfortunate because it has led to serious injury when opposing fans have become destructive, particularly among European soccer fans. But unsportsmanlike conduct encompasses the entire gamut of the sports entertainment industry, including the pampered athletes themselves, their undisciplined coaching staffs, unruly fans, uncivil sports writers and the sponsors whose advertising reflects this "win at all costs" and "in your face" attitude towards the public at large. Taunting left uncontrolled, whether it be performed by one screaming athlete to another or written on the sports pages of America, fosters anger and revenge, and further incites the crowds.

We've begun to recognize that this anger must be controlled. Some sports ruling bodies are trying to regulate behavior among their athletes. For example, college football players are no longer allowed to take their helmets off while on the playing field to taunt their opponents. Professional football has eliminated end zone celebrations after scoring in an attempt to tone down the fan exuberance, particularly among those spun up on alcohol. Some high schools won't tolerate fan disruptions and will forcibly remove those offending fans from the game. And even some community sports leagues have posted signs to remind the parents that their children are watching their behavior.

These are good signs to be sure, but do they go far enough? Or are they just token gestures to present the appearance of trying to regulate unsportsmanlike behavior by athletes?

I believe a lot more can be done. For example, issuing a minuscule fine to a multimillionaire professional athlete does not get his attention and will probably not change his behavior. But issuing a lengthy suspension coupled with a meaningful fine might well be a wake-up call.

It apparently has worked so far for Latrell Sprewell.

There is nothing more sacred to the athlete than playing time. That's his chance to excel. That's his chance to become popular in school. That's his chance in a limited season to get the attention of the college recruiters or the professional scouts. A suspension is the equivalent of taking car privileges away from a teenager—certainly the most important asset to his or her freedom and mobility.

I'm not suggesting taking the fun out of the game, nor ending the competitive spirit. But if pampered athletes truly got punished for their inappropriate and unsportsmanlike behavior, they wouldn't necessarily think of themselves as so very special. They would realize that bad behavior has consequences for them personally and perhaps for the team. If coaches put the fear of suspension for bad behavior as a top priority, then athletes would soon learn the team is more important than the individual. If unruly fans were removed from games, they would soon learn that if they desire to watch their children play, they must be better role models themselves or else forfeit their ticket! If sports writers could write meaningful and factual articles without the use of dishonest, misleading or taunting phrases and name calling, that would go a long way toward improving the civility in fanatic fans who devour every word written about the enemy. And finally, if the leagues would disassociate themselves from sponsors who continue the "in your face" advertising, then sponsors would soon seek more civil ways to promote their products without having to resort to rude and offensive attitudes.

Collegiate athletics in recent years has taken on a new face. It has become big business! Outstanding coaches get paid six and even seven digit salaries and are expected to bring in top recruits to bring in even more money for the school. The student body becomes fanatical over their school spirit. But the lure of more and more money doesn't always support the notion of sportsmanship. College coaches are reluctant to discipline highly talented and pampered athletes, for putting them on the bench jeopardizes their own chances of winning the game or the tournament.

I'm not impugning all coaches or teams. There are several schools that are known for their discipline, and Penn State with longtime football coach Joe Paterno immediately comes to mind. However, there are other schools with the opposite reputation. Here in the state of Florida, with three big time college football rivalries among the University of Florida, Florida State and the University of Miami, there clearly is a difference among these schools in reputation for effective disciplinary action—according to the sports writers in the state. But I'll let you decide where you think the three head coaches rank their support of meaningful disciplinary action. As you rank them, be sure to consider that disciplinary action ought to be for both on and off field infractions, if we expect sports to fulfill their purpose.

If we regulate sportsmanship in the name of safety (clipping, piling on, roughing the kicker) shouldn't we also regulate sportsmanship in the name of civility? Why not?

We regulate behavior all the time. Our jails are full of people who have "misbehaved" or disobeyed the laws we enacted to protect people from injury or death. Why, we even have "quiet" policies in public libraries and movie theaters to regulate rudeness. So why can't we regulate unsportsmanlike conduct? The counter claim, of course, is to emphatically insist that we cannot regulate morals in sports.

Oh really?

We already do! But we use the term "misbehavior" or "unsportsmanlike conduct" rather than the broader definition of morals, which means principles or standards with respect to right and wrong conduct. For example, we don't allow athletes to use profanity or obscene gestures without escaping some form of punishment. We call penalties for flagrant fouls. We eject players and coaches for inappropriate behavior. We even remove unruly or intoxicated fans for the same reason—misbehavior! We even try to regulate behavior by policy, the way some stadiums don't serve beer after the seventh inning or the third quarter.

If we could only find a way to do something to regulate the ornery sports writers!

But we can do more than just complain about the unruly spectators at sporting events. We can insist upon civil behavior. We don't have to accept the guy one row above us constantly spilling beer on our heads, or the guy sitting next to our children who belts out profanity right and left. We need to demand that stadium management promulgate and enforce "sportsmanship" rules for the price of admission and that receipt of a ticket is your consent to agree to those rules. Most people with whom I attend games would heartily endorse these solutions. Only the drunks and those individuals who think that, because they bought a ticket, they are entitled to do whatever they like, would be offended by these constraints on their behavior.

Therefore, shouldn't we demand that we put the emphasis of sportsmanship back into sports? I never hear that term used much today. It has almost left our vocabulary. But its renewed purpose would go a long way toward improving our civility to one another. Perhaps other than music, film and television, amateur and professional sports are one of the most widely watched entertainment events in the nation, and no doubt have a uniquely profound influence on the way we act, as few other institutions outside of church do.

If we could get the millions and millions of fans, executives, athletes, sponsors and sports leagues involved in renewing the purpose of sportsmanship, the term would finally mean something to us again.

*"There is but one uncondi-
tional commandment, which is
that we should seek inces-
santly, with fear and trem-
bling, so to vote and act as to
bring about the very largest
total universe of good which
we can see."*
William James
***The Moral Philosopher
and the Moral Life, 1890***

Chapter 17: The Purpose of Voting

**The purpose of voting is to allow citizens to make
a choice of the elected officials that they desire to
represent them in government business.**

There are many forms of government throughout the
world, but none that compare to the freedoms that exist
in a democracy. A democracy is a form of government
where the majority rules for the common good. It is a
form of government run by the people and for the people,
allowing the populace to change its government

representatives by the mere act of punching a ticket in the voting booth.

In America, we have a representative form of government where the people elect to office individuals who best represent their own economic, political or social views. Theoretically, if that representative falls out of favor with the electorate, another will take his or her place during the next election. At least that is how it is supposed to work.

The secret to the success of the system is the ballot box. The populace must exercise its right to vote in the primaries and the general election. But this seemingly easy task to do, spending a mere few minutes in a voting booth at the local polling precinct, has become one of the most difficult tasks for the average American citizen to accomplish.

In 1996, according to the Federal Election Commission, only 49 percent of the voting age population turned out to vote in the Presidential election (meaning that only one-quarter of the population voted for President Clinton).

Why was that?

Was it complacency? Was it laziness? Was it a lack of knowledge of the candidates and their stand on the issues? Or was it the "my vote doesn't count" syndrome?

It's all of the above.

We have become complacent, choosing instead to whine about our plight in life and the poor performance exhibited by our local, state and federal politicians, rather than deciding to go out and vote them out of office. That's all it takes: punch a ticket in the voting booth, and, bingo, they're gone!

It's not that easy of course, but it's not rocket science either.

Many would have us believe that the real problem is

campaign finance reform. It is a problem of monumental proportions, but the politicians crying the hardest about this issue are doing so for their own agendas. Even if campaign financing were fixed, the real problem would remain--getting people out to vote.

The government has made it extremely easy to register to vote. The new Voting Rights Act enacted in 1993 was supposed to increase voter registration. I believe by most accounts it has. But it hasn't increased voter turnout. We've nearly forced people to register, but that hasn't translated to actual votes.

Most businesses I know allow people time off to go vote, thus avoiding having to use personal time to do one's civic duty. In addition, most polls open early and close late to allow citizens the time needed to exercise their freedoms.

So why can't we get people to vote if we can register them?

Alan Gerber, Professor of Political Science at Yale University, says we can. He conducted a study in Connecticut and determined that "get out the vote" organizations work. He found that 59 percent of those people in Connecticut who were actually contacted did in fact vote.

These are exciting numbers.

According to Rick Hampson in *The Invisible Voter is Everywhere*, seniors are much more inclined to vote than the 18 to 29-year olds. Registered voters with a higher education or more affluence are also more inclined to vote.

In addition, he found that whites are more likely than blacks or Hispanics to vote. If we believe these studies, it seems very logical that we ought to target those groups of people by age, education, economics or heritage who are not inclined to vote, and the number of citizens going to the polls should increase. But it hasn't increased. In fact voter turnout has been declining for decades.

The latest example is our dismal showing in the 1998 elections. Statewide voter turnout percentages for local races were less than 18 percent, the lowest voter turnout rate in our history.

Our congressional races fared a little better by doubling the voter turnout percentages of our statewide races, but they have still remained dismally low, at about 37 percent since 1986. The Federal Election Commission reports on the Internet that turnout for the 1998 Congressional and Senate races in some states—notably Mississippi, Tennessee, Texas, and West Virginia—was as low as 25 percent of the voting age population.

Congressional races during a presidential election year always improve the turnout, but fell for the first time below the 50 percent mark in 1992 (42.9 percent) and again in 1996 (49.2 percent).

This is a national disgrace.

We are proud to tell foreigners that America is "the land of the free and the home of the brave," yet we cannot come close to the 21 Western European democracies who consistently have greater voter turnout percentages than America.

Although we're proud to say we are a democracy, we cannot even conduct the *only* civic responsibility that allows the people a voice in their government and the right to decide who should represent them at all levels of government. Once again, we let other people decide for us. It's what I have been preaching all along about being a critical thinker and getting involved in the purpose of governing.

Here are some interesting facts from the Committee for the Study of the American Electorate. They have estimated that approximately 200 million Americans are among the voting age population and that about 64 percent were registered to vote in 1998. This does not include the approximately 14 million undocumented aliens and the three to four million convicted felons who have lost the privilege (not right) to vote.

The Center for Voting and Democracy lists the following statistics for the 1998 House of Representatives elections. Over 98 percent of the 401 incumbents running for another term of office were reelected. That's right, only six incumbents were defeated - the second highest incumbency reelection rate in our history. Those six who lost were either freshmen or sophomores trying to remain in office; none was an entrenched politician. These are startling numbers. Even more amazing was the fact that 94 House seats were uncontested. In a country with hundreds of millions of people, it should be possible to find 94 qualified to compete against the entrenched incumbents.

Of course it is very easy for us to rationalize our excuse not to vote. "It doesn't matter, all of the politicians from both parties are crooked anyway," we conclude. "Besides, what difference does it make? The Democrats are the same as the Republicans." Or (my favorite), "Well, my vote won't count anyway."

Amazing power can be exhibited by the party which gets out the vote. In 1992 for example, with less than half the voting population going to the polls, Bill Clinton won the presidency with less than a majority of the popular vote. He won again in 1996 with only 49 percent of the electorate voting. As noted earlier, this means that only one-quarter of the voting age citizens of America voted for Bill Clinton! Another 25 percent voted for Bob Dole and Ross Perot, and the rest—nearly 100 million people—just stayed home! That suggests to me that we don't really care about the issues of the day or about who governs us.

Someplace in all of this there remains a mystery. Talk radio and other media outlets loudly proclaim that the public is dissatisfied. The Internet is filled with conspiracy theorists and militia groups angry with government.

How then can we be so regularly showing satisfaction with our elected officials by failing to vote them out of office while at the same time complaining vigorously about governmental policies?

It doesn't make any sense to me.

My view is that most Americans are uninformed, and having little knowledge of their civic responsibility, they refuse to get involved. Most have not developed the critical thinking skills necessary to enable them to decipher all the dishonest rhetoric that emanates out of both political parties.

They get so confused, so dismayed, that they feel it is just not worth the effort.

Because we cannot seem to motivate the electorate to go to the polls, there have been many attempts at persuading the legislatures to revise or devise new voting methods to ensure that all of us are represented fairly. But let's be careful.

Although "proportional representation" is not new among democracies in the world, it is not very common among American state legislatures and city councils. The idea is to provide proportional representation based upon--you guessed it—a quota system.

Minority groups which have been denied their representation because the winner takes all in majority voting, would get representation based on statistics, not votes.

This suggestion is very similar to redistricting to ensure that one party wins over the other by drawing district lines along Democratic, Republican or minority demographics. That practice is called gerrymandering, and it has come under scrutiny by the courts as being unconstitutional.

What does this effort really mean? Doesn't this sound like a new variation of political correctness?

Gerrymandering, redistricting or proportional representation all suggest that because your skin is of a different color, or your philosophy is liberal instead of conservative, you cannot possibly represent me fairly. Therefore, the assumption continues, we must change voting district lines or add representatives, to ensure that we are represented by a person with similar beliefs or looks.

Where does it end? Should this concept apply to women (who, by the way, are in the majority) and to different ethnic and religious groups also?

Proportional representation can only add to the cost of government. Creating more legislators and their staffs in the apparent belief that skin color or ethnicity is the only fair way to represent constituents is just one more way to divide this country.

This is only one more example of how far we've drifted from our historical roots. These new approaches are not inclusive, but divisive.

Another cry one often hears is from third party candidates, their staff or their constituents, who claim it is very difficult for them even to get invited to the debate; and therefore it is almost impossible for them to upset the two major party candidates, particularly at the national level. But Governor Jesse Ventura did beat the odds in 1998 at the state level. He won the governor's race in Minnesota over two challengers who carried well-known political family names from the Republican and Democratic parties.

Governor Ventura won the election with one of the

largest voter turnouts in the nation in 1998. So the
question we must ask is why did Minnesota voters turn
out to vote in a much larger percentage of the voting age
electorate than the rest of the nation? Was it because
Minnesota was tired of the same old politics from the
Democrats and the Republicans? Was it that Jesse
Ventura, a former Navy SEAL and pro wrestler and a small
town Mayor, possessed celebrity status? Or did he offer
better solutions than his opponents on the issues affecting
the voters? Or did the voters think that Jesse Ventura
offered the best hope for Minnesotans to recapture the
integrity of the office with the character issue? Could the
electorate have chosen character over issues?

Vice Admiral James B. Stockdale, a true American
hero, prisoner-of-war and national leader, has advocated
for years that "character over issues" ought to be one of
the main concerns in the electorate's mind when they enter
the voting booth. He argues persuasively that issues are
transient, and often change as soon as the politician is in
office. On the other hand, he says that "character is
forever." As I have stated in previous chapters, character
is a reflection of who you are, what you are all about and
how you conduct yourself in both the public and the private
domain. The public and the private domain are inseparable
when it comes to character! It is therefore realistic to
believe that if you vote for character, based upon principle,
integrity and honesty, you will certainly be voting for a
candidate who will govern the same way he campaigns.

Unfortunately, we have many candidates today who
lack integrity and will say and do anything to become
elected, and then vote their ideological philosophy
regardless of their previous stance.
So, back to the question! Why did Jesse Ventura win
the governor's office in Minnesota? I believe it was because

the voters truly wanted a change and sought the celebrity status of Jesse Ventura whom they believed provided them with straight talk on the issues. I am convinced however, that they never even considered character over issues in their voting decisions.

Do you recall the recent, widely reported *Playboy Magazine* interview where Governor Ventura took a swipe at the faithful? He claimed those people who belonged to an organized religion were weak and needed organized religion as a crutch. How can a man of character and integrity say such an outrageous statement and offend a majority of Americans in the process? Particularly interesting is that he considers those who attend an organized religious activity as weak, but does not consider those who attend a phony, organized wrestling match as weak. If churchgoers are considered weak because they prefer to gather together for inspiration, then wrestling audiences who gather for entertainment must be equally as weak. I don't get it! The Governor ought to understand that the faithful who go to church and the fans who attend wrestling matches do so for a purpose; one is to pray, the other is to be entertained. But to claim that organized religion is for the weak is to fail to understand religion's purpose.

But back to character. Governor Ventura's polling numbers dropped 19 points immediately following his remarks. I wonder if the good people of Minnesota who voted for Governor Ventura still find him attractive today. Or do they now find his character a little wanting? I'm not impugning Governor Ventura or his constituents, but merely pointing out that character is as important a trait in the candidates who represent us in government as is their basic philosophy of life.

Perhaps this was hindsight in Jesse Ventura's case,

but what about the many people (although not a majority) who still voted for Bill Clinton for President despite the fact that it was widely reported while he was Arkansas' Attorney General, and later its Governor, that he possessed serious character flaws. The point to remember is that if your vote is based on character and honesty and integrity, you will most likely be governed with principle, as opposed to haphazard governing by those who are opportunistic and who sought the office for personal gain.

So, what is the solution?

The nation needs to refocus its efforts on voter turnout during the year 2000 elections, as we see has already happened with the Republican primaries.

We need to actively support "get out the vote" drives and become *involved* in the process.

We need to understand once again the *purpose* of voting in a democracy where majority rules.

There is no other way for the nation to remain a democracy in the new millennium.

*"The Word was made
flesh, and dwelt among us ...
full of grace and truth."*
The Holy Bible
John 1:14

Chapter 18: The Purpose of Truth

***The purpose of truth is to ascertain one's
character and to determine the actual state of affairs.***

Most children grow up believing that "honesty is the best policy," or at least it was that way when I was a child. I learned that George Washington couldn't tell a lie and therefore admitted to his father that he chopped down the cherry tree. I don't really know if this story (or myth) is true, but it sends the right message to impressionable youngsters.

There are some historians today who want to revise this story and history as well, for their own personal agendas, regardless of whether there is moral value behind their tale. The George Washington story is an innocent one, and regardless of its truth, it has no far reaching consequences except in the revision, which reduces the stature of the first president of the United States.

But far more disturbing than the revision of something as innocuous as the cherry tree story is the implication of the revision itself. The message is clear: honesty is no longer valued as it once was.

Our justice system, once the great equalizer of good versus evil, is in disarray. Truth or consequences is not necessarily the rule applied today. As children, we always knew that the "good guys" would prevail. We understood that Eliot Ness would beat the "bad guys", and that the local sheriff would catch the bank robbers. We instinctively knew that good would triumph over evil, and the theater and television portrayals of courtroom justice at that time bore witness: the good guys always locked up the bad guys.

We acknowledged that certain standards of acceptable behavior were required for a society to maintain law and order, and we instinctively understood that misbehavior would have serious consequences. The concept of "swearing to tell the truth, the whole truth and nothing but the truth so help me God," in a court of law was practically part of our folklore. We all knew what that phrase meant. But something happened to our culture along the way. Something that has turned truth seeking upside down. Courts of law, committee hearings, political activities and corporate boardrooms now seek the goal of winning for the sake of ideology or personal agendas rather than for the purpose of revealing the whole truth.

The new agendas which hold little regard for truth telling vary from ideology (Clinton's impeachment), to racism (the second trial for police officers acquitted in the first Rodney King trial), to greed (state tobacco lawsuits), to ignoring the evidence while attacking the process (O. J.

Simpson's criminal trial). In each of these celebrated cases it was all about winning for a personal agenda versus seeking the truth.

A few examples:

Ideology prevented many liberal Democrats from denouncing the President's personal behavior, for which most of us would have lost our jobs and quite possibly have gone to jail. Today, most people agree that the President perjured himself—as does the judge who found President Clinton in contempt of court and fined him appropriately.

Protest marches and cries of racism caused the government to seek a new trial and not accept the police officers' acquittal by a jury of their peers in the first Rodney King beating trial. The government succeeded in ordering a new trial under a new jurisdiction, all for the sake of quelling the disturbances in Los Angeles.

Greed, not common sense and a review of the facts, caused the state's Attorneys General to file huge claims against the tobacco companies seeking enormous profits for the state's coffers (and the individual attorneys themselves), despite the many years of government mandated labeling of the hazards of smoking. Should the government now be sued by the tobacco companies for their failure years earlier to ensure a much stronger label be placed on their cigarette packaging and therefore eliminate cigarette smoking and death altogether?

In complete disregard of the mountain of evidence, including DNA samples, against O. J. Simpson in his criminal trial, winning at all costs by attacking the prosecution and the police versus defending the motives of the accused, ruled the trial proceedings. Seeking the truth never seemed to be the purpose of the defense.

Winning, even if dishonestly, has become the primary

focus for many prosecutors and defense attorneys. In order to bolster their cases, they often will not offer relevant evidence at trial if it hurts their client's chances for either acquittal or conviction. But morally, how can we either defend a criminal who has committed a horrendous crime against humanity or conversely convict an innocent person simply to win a case? Aren't we morally obligated to society to do the right thing and seek the truth based upon the merit of the evidence? And if that evidence leads us to fail in our attempt to either vindicate or convict the accused, isn't that what we should be striving for, regardless of our personal agendas? Are we truly so arrogant that we cannot accept defeat if the truth were told, regardless of our position? And if the verdict by the jury is so unpopular that it is met with protest marches, is the government really obligated to file additional charges or seek the intervention of other jurisdictions or higher courts? Isn't that considered double jeopardy, just to win a favorable ruling?

Judges and jurors—supposedly the defenders of blind justice—labor under the same ideology and personal agendas as the rest of us. Instead, shouldn't they be seeking the truth, rather than displaying partisan thoughts and feelings in misguided attempts to justify the failings of our cultural past? Seeking the truth based upon established fact no longer seems to be the purpose of modern juries. Juries today are sympathetic to John Q. Citizen and award huge compensatory and punitive damages in class action suits against deep-pocket corporations. Juries seem to go by their feelings rather than evidence. Why else would they award huge amounts of money to smokers when in fact the government required cigarette manufacturers to display health hazards as labels on cigarette packaging for many years. When partisan jurors lack the critical thinking skills required to render a proper verdict based upon the truth, justice is not served.

The current Justice Department has failed in its mission. Once revered as the government agency that would ensure equal justice under the law, it finds itself today embroiled in controversy that runs the gamut from inadequate law enforcement, to sloppy investigating, to poor courtroom justice. Its original purpose, which remains valid today, is to enforce the laws on the books to ensure justice prevails no matter the characterization of the alleged crime. Justice seeks the truth in order to punish the guilty and acquit the innocent, no matter the color, gender, nationality, wealth, power, or prestige of the accused. In other words, justice should be blind! But is it?

The justice system was politicized early in the Clinton Administration when all the U.S. Attorneys were asked to resign - an act that never before had been done. And clearly there was only one purpose in doing so, and that was to get Clinton appointees in every jurisdiction in the United States. So ideology first appeared in the judicial system en masse in the early part of the last decade.

And later, still more politicizing from the Reno Justice Department occurred when the common practice of randomly selecting and rotating judges to preside over cases was abandoned in favor of handpicking judges to match the outcome the Department was hoping for. Does this appear to be "blind justice" when the Justice Department hand picks the judge? This practice is particularly corrupting in high profile cases where ideology, race, greed and fame play a role and in which high priced and well-connected lawyers see that their celebrity clients get preferential treatment.

The justice system in the United States needs to refocus its efforts on seeking the truth. The American Bar

Association and the Trial Lawyers of America ought to take seriously their role in improving law enforcement efforts and courtroom behavior to fight crime. They need to review their purpose as an association and stop trying to federalize every criminal act in an attempt to demonstrate to the public that they are serious about crime. Laws on the books serve no purpose unless they are enforced. In addition, the Bar Association and the Trial Lawyers need to police their own ranks to discipline lawyers and judges who violate courtroom procedures. They need to disbar those attorneys who commit felonies or misdemeanors.

The real difficulty in seeking the truth today is in defining accountability. The fundamental question used to be, who was responsible for the crime? But judges and jurors now are notoriously famous for disregarding accountability. They often allege conspiracies where there are none. Lawyers seeking to confuse the issue or attack the process deliberately mislead their juries. The accused is often portrayed as the victim. Sound familiar? Judges and jurors should just ask these simple questions: who was responsible for the crime? What was their motive? Does the evidence lead me to a specific conclusion? Judges and jurors need to understand their purpose is to seek the truth, not to convey their personal agendas or ideology to reach a verdict. They need to be critical thinkers, not sympathetic ideologues.

Truthfulness for many Americans is no longer a virtue. It is not uncommon for people to stretch the truth, mislead, even lie or perjure themselves without feeling the slightest remorse, shame or guilt. As a nation, we have lost the "fear factor" in our lives. It just doesn't matter to some if they get caught lying. They will just rationalize a response that blames someone or something else for their mistake.
Why is there no embarrassment, no guilt, no shame,

for this routine disrespect for the truth?

I contend that because we suffer no consequences, we no longer fear mistakes. And if we do suffer consequences, we sue the company or our employer for the oddest of reasons imaginable—stress on the job, inadequate training to do the job, discrimination, racism. Take for example a case currently before the U.S. Supreme Court, which will decide whether millions of Americans who own cars built before air bags became mandatory (it was optional), can sue automakers for not installing them. It apparently doesn't matter if the driver was at fault, or the government wasn't smart enough to pass mandatory air bag laws in the '40s, or the automaker executives didn't have the foresight earlier to voluntarily put air bags into automobiles. No, what matters to greedy lawyers is to turn back the clock on decision making and claim neglect!

What's next? Will we see the clock turned back on boating accidents because we have yet to invent, design or deploy an operational air bag or an automatically inflated safety vest which will save human lives in the future? If the U.S. Supreme Court decides favorably for the plaintiffs in these types of negligence suits, then by the same logic, I think the automakers' lawyers should sue the government, particularly Congress, for not passing the air bag laws sooner.

Where does this idiocy end? The truth is, judges, juries and lawyers have gone far beyond the mandate set for them some 200 years ago by our Founding Fathers. Greed—not truth and justice—rules today's courtrooms.

What is truly distressing is the fact that few public officials today are held accountable for their misdeeds, particularly when the infraction is dishonesty. It appears that dishonesty to cover up a more serious offense gets more play than the actual crime itself. Lawyers are good at deflecting the serious charges and down playing the dishonesty by claiming that their client's deception was just a matter of interpretation. Parsing of words, made famous by our President, is seen as a serious attempt to explain why there could have been a misinterpretation of the events. Therefore, let's forgive him for his mistake because anybody could have misconstrued the comment. And meanwhile, the more serious crime of perjury (lying under oath) is forgotten.

But what have we done here? The United States justice system is based on the premise that everybody is innocent until proven guilty. If accused, you are allowed your day in court unless you waive those rights. Assuming you have your day in court, our system relies on the truth, the whole truth and nothing but the truth. Officials of the court are sworn in, and every witness, with hand on a bible, swears under oath before God to tell the whole truth. Truth is the cornerstone of the judicial system, and we rely upon truth telling to support the evidence. So, if we lie to the court (commit perjury), we have undermined the fairness of the verdict in the case.

But truth telling is not just a pillar of the judicial system. It is the *cornerstone* to every relationship we enjoy. Telling the truth is a fundamental indication of character. Truth telling is a reflection of who we are—it goes right to the heart of our integrity. And if we make a mistake and try to cover it up by lying, we demonstrate a serious character flaw that reflects our inability to accept our failures.

But if we admit a mistake and stand up to principle, regardless of the consequences, we have shown true character and the ability to accept our faults. Let's remember that people make mistakes all the time. After all, we are only human. But let's also remember that we expect people to tell the truth and admit when they are wrong. For without the truth there can be no trust, and without trust, there can be no civility. In a civilized society there is no other way!

The purpose behind telling the truth is self-evident. It goes to the very heart of the rule of law. For without truth we cannot properly render a judgment, and without the rule of law to guide us in our decision making, "feelings" underscore our ability to ensure equal justice for all.

The United States of America is a democratic republic with a justice system based upon a sound principle of the rule of law. That means that the law applies to everyone equally, regardless of status in life. No one should be allowed to circumvent the law because of power, wealth, prestige or celebrity status. And of course there are avenues for appeals, and stays, but why the fuss over issues that are clearly for the courts, juries and the rule of law to decide? Feelings and emotions should play no part in the equal justice under the law provision.

But that's exactly what is happening in South Florida over the decision to send little six-year-old Elian Gonzalez back to Cuba. He is the little boy who survived a boat wreck only to lose his mother and ten others at sea. Elian is now at the center of an international tug-of-war between the Castro government and his father's right to custody on one side; and the largely Hispanic population in South Florida who are seeking asylum or adoption of the boy to allow him to remain in the United States on the other.

This unfortunately is being touted as the boy's rights under the constitution to be allowed to remain in the United States. However, there is no constitutional right for an illegal immigrant to remain in the United States, no matter his age. There is a constitutional right to equal justice under the law, and a right to be heard in the courts. But once the court decides, based upon the rule of law (and not on "emotion"), then the protesters and family members on both sides of the issue need to comply with the court's decision.

But, this issue has gone way beyond reason at this point. The hysteria in South Florida is simply about ideology versus the rule of law. It is about emotions (hatred for the Cuban government) and not about justice under our immigration and naturalization laws. There would be no protests in the streets of Miami if this issue were simply about the rule of law. Everybody would understand that the courts must decide the issue, one way or the other. But these protests, stirred up by the hatred of the anti-Castro advocates, have caused us all to believe that this is about freedom for the boy versus returning him to a communist nation. But in fact, this is about a father's rights to custody under the American rule of law.

Many Americans sympathize with the ideal to seek freedom and assume that what is best for the boy is to live in a democracy. And that certainly is a worthy cause. However, as a parent, under American law, Elian's father has the right (unless taken from him by the courts for being an abusive father) to reclaim the boy he almost lost at sea. And certainly Fidel Castro ought to let the father come to the United States to take his son home, if he chooses to do so. How arrogant of the people of South Florida (the anti-Castro crowd) and others to tell a Cuban father that they know what is best for his son, simply because he lives in communist Cuba. They say freedom is far more important to the child than oppression in his homeland. But they don't know that. Right now Elian is being treated as a mini-hero in Havana. Why would they oppress him with all the international attention?

But let's change the story somewhat. Would we hear the same outcry if the father had died trying to sail to America while the mother was left behind in Cuba and claimed she wanted her son returned to her? It's very difficult for Americans to deny a mother the right to nurture her child, but it is amazingly easy to forget a father's right, simply because the parents have divorced or separated. I'm guessing there would be much less fuss over this issue if the roles were reversed because the media would have played the father as a kidnapper, denying the mother her rights to visit with her son.

And of course we would be as outraged as the people in Havana have become over Elian Gonzalez' detention, if an American boy of six was rescued and detained in the home of Cuban relatives and was not being allowed to be returned to his natural father in Florida.

But let's all remember Elian still has a natural father and the United States still operates under the rule of law. If the people in South Florida don't like the ultimate decision to be rendered by the court, then they should go to the polls or lobby their representatives and change the law, but don't abuse it! I continue to believe that when we personalize any situation, most clear thinking Americans can understand the father's right to custody, as the national polls on this issue suggest.

While the appeal process is underway, the federal government needs to decide which court has jurisdiction over this case - federal or state. Attorney General Janet Reno has recently ruled that federal immigration and naturalization laws take precedence over the state court, but my guess is that this case will end up in the Supreme Court because Congress will hold hearings and delay the decision without regard to the rule of law. Meanwhile, the

protestors in South Florida need to await the final decision
rather than call for civil disobedience over an issue that is
clearly for the courts to decide.

"When an American says he loves his country, he means not only that he loves the New England hills, the prairies glistening in the sun, the wide and rising plains, the great mountains and the sea. He means he loves an inner air, an inner light in which freedom lives and in which a man can draw the breath of self-respect."
Governor Adlai Stevenson, 1952 speech to the Democratic National Convention

Chapter 19: The Purpose of Patriotism

The purpose of patriotism is to foster a deep love of country that unites the citizenry in a common goal to defend the principles for which it stands.

Our country was founded on the principles of democracy and freedom. We no longer wanted to be governed by the Crown, but by elected representatives. We no longer wanted to belong to the Church of England, but to be able to worship as we wish. We no longer would tolerate taxation without representation. We were fed up with sending our hard-earned money across the Atlantic for interests the English Monarchy decided were best.

We declared our country an independent nation in

1776 because we demanded a representative government that would listen to the people. We demanded freedom in our newfound country to decide for ourselves how we should be taxed and governed; and how we should pray and educate our children. We chose candidates who best represented our own political and philosophical views. We chose churches or synagogues that best reflected our own moral beliefs and upbringing. We established an enduring Constitution with a Bill of Rights that best expressed our views of how we were to be governed as a people, by the people and for the people, without fear of retribution from the very government we were establishing.

Those principles remain relevant today, and that is why I call myself a patriot. It's not because I served in the United States Navy, nor because I fought in two wars defending my country's interests; it's because I believe in the principles our Constitution stands for — democracy, freedom and a representative form of government. Most Americans share this belief, but many are not convinced we are headed in the right direction. Some, including the far right militias sprouting up all over the country, have grave misgivings concerning the method in which our government is slowly removing the freedoms we fought so hard to win more than two hundred years ago. But we ought not to condemn them as unpatriotic, as the liberal press often does. In an ironic twist, the same liberal press defends other citizens who would rather live under a socialistic or communistic government, as their pronouncements are declared "freedom of speech." Certainly any militia or communist group that advocates the overthrow of our government ought to be condemned for being unpatriotic, and should be brought to justice legally.

A patriot is defined as someone who loves and defends

his or her country. The term doesn't necessarily refer to the military only. A patriot is one willing to defend the ideals his country stands for. That is why the Fourth of July always evokes a patriotic mood. It is because the citizenry is celebrating the nation's birthday and the ideals of freedom and democracy. Parades with banners and flags and marching music stir the emotions. Speeches recall a vibrant history. Everywhere you look on the Fourth of July you witness patriotism in the form of military marching bands and precision drill teams performing in local festivities. The American flag, the symbol of our great nation, flies proudly atop our state and federal buildings and on numerous flagpoles and houses, boats and cars throughout the land. Patriotic music abounds on the airwaves. John Philip Souza inspires us to feel good about ourselves and our country.

Patriotism is a feeling that absorbs me and many other Americans who feel as I do, that the greatness of this country's history, ideals and principles requires us to remain true to its cause. If you are like me, and understand our history and why America declared independence from the British almost two hundred and twenty-four years ago, you will truly appreciate the freedoms we enjoy and the importance of the great ideals embodied in our Declaration of Independence, the Constitution and the Bill of Rights. You also understand the purpose for our existence and you believe that its purpose is right. Can you imagine the euphoria on July 4, 1776, when we became a free nation with the right to determine our own way of life via a democratic process? We cannot let that feeling die. We must restore that patriotic feeling even though we have flaws as a nation.

My view is that many Americans accept their government for what it is, but show no emotion for its purpose one way or the other. I equate this lack of emotional feeling as a lack of commitment. It is the same reason some companies, or sports teams or schools lack an emotional spirit, because they just don't understand what it means to commit to an ideal. When you are completely committed to someone or something, you are passionate about supporting them. Commitment is the key, and patriotism towards your country is based upon the same commitment to country as team spirit or school spirit is to the team or the school. Without a commitment for the ideals they stand for, the ultimate result is a lack of common purpose.

I suspect that many Americans fall into this category. They are not committed because they feel their government is just not committed to them. But patriotism is love of country, not love of government. It is hard to commit yourself to defending its ideals without fully supporting the machinery of government. For example, I am incensed at the way our government operates today. I'm incensed over our "morally challenged" President. However, despite that feeling of moral outrage, I am an American full of pride in America, the beautiful. I love my country, "for which it stands: one nation, under God, indivisible with liberty and justice for all." If you sing the words to the "Star Spangled Banner" or "America the Beautiful" and don't become emotional over them, tear up or get goose bumps, then perhaps you need a dose of patriotism. Perhaps you need a dose of commitment. If you don't stand as the flag passes by or place your hand over your heart, or if you are not deeply troubled when a citizen burns our flag, then perhaps you need to be reminded of the purpose of patriotism.

On the other hand, do you feel there should be a Constitutional amendment to declare flag burning a federal offense? I'm incensed that any citizen would desecrate the flag that symbolizes America, but because the government should not be in the business of federalizing ideology or stupidity, I'm not for a Constitutional amendment to make it a federal offense. We fought hard for the right to express ourselves freely. And although I don't consider the burning of our flag to be an example of free speech, as some claim, it is a *freedom of expression.*

Think of the lawsuits that will surely arise over this proposed amendment. Is it legal to burn the American flag in your own house, or on your patio or in your front yard, but not on a public street or in a public park? Can the Feds come and grab you on your own property just to stop you from burning a flag that you bought and own? What about burning a sheet of music with the words for "The Star Spangled Banner" or a copy of the Constitution, Declaration of Independence or Pledge of Allegiance? Where will it end? The act may incense me, but a Constitutional amendment is the wrong avenue to pursue. How about a fine for outdoor burning without a license?

I'm not suggesting that most Americans want to rewrite our Constitution or do away with our republican form of government. Rather, I'm suggesting that we return to our roots and allow the people to decide how to govern themselves without federalizing every crime, without removing states' rights reserved solely to them in the Constitution itself, and without mandating policy via executive order, judicial fiat or regulatory directive. Even with all our flaws as a nation, we enjoy more freedoms than any other country in the world, and we have more opportunities than any other country in the world. All we need to do is remember them and take advantage of them.

In the end, the way we live our lives is a matter of commitment; it is the key to happiness. If we commit ourselves to God, country and family, I guarantee we will be happy with our lot in life. That doesn't mean there won't be challenges, but it does mean that we will be satisfied with our effort, knowing we stood by our principles without faltering.

Let's not be "situational patriots" who only become patriotic on the Fourth of July as we celebrate our nation's birthday in a special way. Let's be patriotic all year, because deep down we believe in our way of life, our democratic process and our freedom of the press, freedom to choose our own religious beliefs, and freedom to vote as we choose.

And let's remember the words of President John F. Kennedy: "Don't ask what your country can do for you, but what you can do for your country." This simple, patriotic phrase, when applied to our family, our neighborhood, our school and our business, can have that same uplifting spirit as intended when President Kennedy proclaimed these words some thirty-five years ago.

Morality, patriotism and commitment are a powerful recipe for happiness and purpose of life. And patriotism is a worthy principle to nourish as our country seeks a way to end its moral drifting.

"But would the honest patriot, in the full tide of successful experiment, abandon a government which has so far kept us free and firm, on the theoretic and visionary fear that this government, the world's best hope, may by possibility want energy to preserve itself?"
Thomas Jefferson

Chapter 20: The Purpose of Hope

The purpose of hope is to instill a feeling that what is wanted will happen.

Do you ever dream? Do you ever think of what the future will hold for you and your family?

It's a natural feeling to hope, just as it is to feel despair.

We all hope for the best. We all wish we could change things in our lives for the better. We all, at some point in our life, dream of the future and how we would like it to be.

But dreaming and wishing are not enough. We must take action and be optimistic. We must learn to enjoy the satisfaction that comes with conquering our fears. We must truly dedicate ourselves to becoming critical thinkers, always looking for the positive about the joys we have at our disposal right now. We must strive to subordinate our negative feelings in order to gain a perspective on what truly matters in our lives.

As the United States of America makes the transition from the twentieth century to the twenty-first, it finds itself in an identity crisis. No longer a nation of one people, one society, the United States is in imminent danger of becoming a nation of many individuals, all seemingly bent on tearing apart their country's soul.

Although the United States is the only remaining superpower in terms of military might and economic power, it is no longer a nation of moral right. Its citizens mistrust each other and judge each other based upon ideology and affiliation, rather than accepting differences of opinion.

Many Americans lack critical thinking skills. Many blindly accept news and analysis as gospel. Instead of reasoned debate, we tend to raise the rhetoric, leading to incivility and violence.

Because of a lack of Presidential moral authority to govern, the country can no longer demand that the world follow our lead. Washington is afloat with powerful politicians—reaching to the highest elected and appointed officials of the land—who are either now or have recently been under indictment or investigation by the Justice Department for a lack of ethics or worse.

Congress is split by ideology and mistrust of each other. An activist Judiciary legislates rather than interprets the law. Governmental bureaucrats and committee staffers, though not elected, run the machinery of government. Nonelected but federally appointed regulators are empowered to make decisions affecting our daily lives, regardless of our wishes. There are so many federal departments, branches, agencies and commissions that the average American has no idea of its breadth and depth.

Our government has become a multilayered monster that is grossly inefficient, duplicating programs at every level down to city councils. We have highly paid lobbyists and activists whose sole purpose is to advocate support for their particular agendas, even if that legislation does not represent the majority view of most Americans.

In addition to an out of control and undisciplined government which has lost its direction and original purpose of being, a host of social ills prevail as well. The dismantling of the family unit has occurred as parents have abrogated their responsibilities toward nurturing their children to adulthood. The populace is overcome by complacency, either due to a robust economy which encourages them to have it all at no thought for future consequences, or because they have simply dropped out in total frustration and despair over the inability to control the bureaucratic maze of regulation and taxation.

The concept of the real purpose of family seems to have eroded nearly past the possibility of repair. We would rather let our children play video games and watch hours of unenlightened television than have them study or sit down at the dinner table and chat. Children grow up by themselves, out of control and under limited supervision. They are not taught civility but rather are allowed to absorb the warped values displayed in video games and puerile cartoons and raunchy sitcoms on television.

Our children idolize idiots, not heroes.

And whom do we blame? Hollywood is the scapegoat, although to blame our entertainment industry is clearly an effort to escape our own responsibility as parents. Because many American parents feel as I do, that Hollywood is out of control, we don't blame Hollywood for our kids idolizing idiots instead of heroes. We take responsibility into our own hands, ensuring that our children focus their attention on proper role models.

Yet, there is a glimmer of hope on the horizon: we are fighting back.

We are filled with anger and frustration, justifiably so.

Religion is suppressed in public for the wrong-headed sake of preserving the Constitution's separation of church and state. We have the nation's public school systems in disarray, begging for more and more money to fix what they have already destroyed by their lack of discipline, lowered standards, cultural diversity and feel-good theories. Schools have become a hotbed for social reform against our wishes. Our education system, although one of the most costly in the industrialized world, ranks among the least effective in the world.

The justice system has been turned upside down by juries which decide penalties based on feelings rather than on the rule of law. Victims of crimes have suffered through endless defense appeals by liberal minded lawyers who feel prisoners are mistreated but who have no similar regard for the victims themselves. Many judges mandate policies based upon ideology rather than merit, without regard to the economic and social havoc those policies wrack upon the citizenry.

The press has been irresponsible when unfairly reporting the news. National reporters have become celebrities who worry more about their salaries than they do about obtaining responsible answers to responsible questions. They have so slanted the news that it is inconceivable to me why most Americans fail to perceive their motives.

With the exception of most of our churches, synagogues and commercial places of work, the institutions that we Americans rely on more than any other in our daily lives have failed to live up to their charters. The over-bloated government, the failed public schools systems and the sleazy entertainment industry have combined surreptitiously to add to our moral decline.

The government has overtaxed us to the point that many households now require two-parent incomes, which means less time nurturing our children. The public school system has "dumbed down" America to the point that our children know more about social issues (a parental responsibility) than they know about vocabulary, reading, critical thinking skills, math, history and science. The entertainment industry has added to the increased violence and incivility of our youth by not emphasizing moral and civil responsibility in television, movie and video game programming.

And because we sense that we cannot quickly change the direction of these powerful institutions, we have become a nation of complacent whiners blaming everything and everybody else but ourselves for our lot in life.

Because we mistakenly believe that money will fix all our ills and allow us to escape reality, our relief from this frustration is to play the lottery or sue big corporations for our own past indiscretions or misuse of their products.

That's the bad news.

The good news is that we are in control, if we want to be.

I believe that we, as individuals and as a nation, can restore our moral authority. We can start by placing a renewed emphasis on the importance of the family unit. We need to teach every child in America that each one has a responsibility to society, and we need to show each one how to go about carrying out that responsibility.

Unless the parents of America unite against the lack of principles and incivility in our neighborhoods and our schools, we will continue to fracture into divisiveness. Our immoral behavior has caused fathers to deny their children, mothers to abort or to abandon them. We have placed our children's care with organizations whose purpose is either to make profits (day care) or teach curriculums (public schools) we don't sanction.

Our word to one another means nothing today. An oath of office and a marriage vow are merely words to mouth, not to live by. Our children's heroes are insolent rap artists or pampered athletes. Their role models are no longer their fathers, because their fathers have gone AWOL.

Civility is a lost art with "in your face" advertising and entertainment programming. We now prefer to put somebody down and ridicule him or her as opposed to trying to persuade the person to our point of view.

Standards have fallen to accommodate feelings.

We pass laws to make ourselves feel better, but we don't enforce them, causing lawlessness to abound everywhere.

We celebrate diversity rather than tolerate it. Our rhetoric has become invective rather than soothing. We no longer believe in principle, but expediency and greed. Discipline is a farce because we don't want to hurt anybody's feelings. Religion is considered extremism, but homosexuality is considered mainstream. Taxes are considered the property of the government rather than money taken from the people to support governing. Character doesn't count because we have determined people should not be judgmental of behavior.

In general, society has imploded under a barrage of attacks on the virtues of common decency. We live passively in a world that has turned upside down the ideals of principle, character and morality.

Nikita Khruschev once predicted that Russia would not have to destroy the United States, because we would do it ourselves. We would fall from within. Nearly forty years later it appears he was more right than wrong.

So what do we intend to do about this?

We can start by being more positive, more optimistic in our daily interactions. Continue to demonstrate to your children, your neighbors and your coworkers that there is a good purpose to life, there is hope in our future. Fight back against incivility by adhering to certain principles of right and wrong and common decency.

Although we may not agree on every issue, we certainly can demand respect for our beliefs.

In my opinion, the only way to survive as a nation is to demonstrate that we stand for certain principles and are committed to a just cause. Without a sense of history we are living for the moment only, and that means we are committed to ourselves as individuals and not to society as a whole.

The Declaration of Independence pulled us together against tyranny and caused us to commit our very lives to the cause of freedom. Do we still have that sense of duty today? Of course we do.

There are many military and civilian men and women serving their country in far off lands, willing to die if need be, to preserve our national interests. At home there are the policemen and firemen and other public safety personnel who daily risk their lives for us. We have thousands of dedicated fathers and mothers who spend time organizing Boy Scouts and Girl Scouts and other community programs. We have religious institutions in every city of the country that provide for the poor, hungry and disheartened among us.

This is what dedication and commitment to something other than ourselves is all about.

The Declaration of Independence is an amazing document. When was the last time you read it? In high school? It's well worth reading again. It's what I call a document of hope.

Do you recall what was written so many years ago? In the early days of the Republic, the nation stood for certain core values. Those values were enumerated in that declaration, which among other things included a statement that "life, liberty and the pursuit of happiness" came from God, not from government. Back then the nation hoped for a better way of life—a way of life committed to certain ideals and freedoms.

We cannot abandon what our forefathers fought for, nor lose our sense of history. We must rededicate ourselves to the Pledge of Allegiance.

Instead of dismay, anger and frustration, why don't we get involved and put America back on its moral path to greatness.

Here's how we can do it, together.

First of all, take control of your life and become a responsible parent. Put discipline back into your children's lives. Show them what principles are all about. Teach them right from wrong. Insist on standards of common decency and good conduct. Take them to church and show them that character really does count.

Secondly, get involved in your local government. Demand a tax cut and an efficiency review of all governmental agencies. Go out and perform your civic duty and vote.

Thirdly, take back your children's education, by peaceful disobedience if necessary, when the establishment does not listen to your concerns for school reform.

Fourthly, boycott the advertisers who put filth into the entertainment world of music, movies and television. If enough of us do it, they will soon get the message.

Fifthly, be a good neighbor and stop the dishonest rhetoric and incivility towards one another. Understand that disagreement with issues is not necessarily intolerance, it's merely expressing a different opinion.

And finally, be optimistic. Dedicate yourself to the common good of society, be hopeful and understand the PURPOSE behind the things we do and say. Learn to become a critical thinker in order to be able to understand the issues affecting your personal life.

And *always* remember that everything around us is done for a PURPOSE, a principle that should no longer be forgotten!

ABOUT THE AUTHOR

A native of Reno, Nevada, Captain Raymond M. Wikstrom completed undergraduate study at the University of Nevada at Reno, in January, 1968. Immediately entering the Navy through Aviation Officer Candidate School in Pensacola, Florida, his first assignment was with the "Seawolves" of Hal-3, located in Bin Thuy, Republic of Vietnam, piloting Huey gunships on more than 600 combat missions.

Upon returning to the United States, Captain Wikstrom served on the USS Intrepid, USS Trippe, USS Bowen, and USS Elmer Montgomery. He also completed a shore duty assignment as instructor pilot at the Jacksonville, Florida, Naval Air Station, and commanded two helicopter squadrons at the nearby Mayport facility.

Following an assignment with the Deputy Chief of Naval Operations Air Warfare staff at the Pentagon, where he was responsible for all Navy helicopter force level planning, he served as the Executive Officer of USS Tripoli before taking over command of the Helicopter Sea Control Wing 3 at the Mayport Naval Station.

At the outbreak of Desert Storm, Captain Wikstrom was the commanding officer of the Amphibious Assault Flagship USS Okinawa in the Persian Gulf. He also commanded the USS Tarawa, before ending his 30-year Naval career back in Washington, D.C., with the Bureau of Naval Personnel.

Captain Wikstrom's personal awards include four Legions of Merit, three Meritorious Service Medals, the Distinguished Flying Cross, the Strike/Flight Air Medal, the Navy and Marine Corps Commendation Medal, and the Spanish Navy Merit Medal First Class.

In 1989 he was the Atlantic Fleet recipient of the prestigious Admiral James B. Stockdale Inspirational Leadership Award.

Captain Wikstrom and his family live in Jacksonville, Florida.